bonsai
life histories

MARTIN TREASURE

bonsai
life histories

FIREFLY BOOKS

acknowledgments

I would like to thank those who have helped me enormously with this book: my editor, Jo Richardson, who was always more than helpful, extremely enthusiastic and incredibly professional; Bet Ayer, whose design skills not only interpreted my ideas but improved them; my wife, Ceri Treasure, the driving force behind this book, for her enthusiasm, encouragement and willingness to accept that the book took up a lot of my time; Lynn Treasure, my mother, for sharing her tremendous excitement and enthusiasm, and for her invaluable advice; my father, Malcolm Treasure, for always encouraging and helping me — never more so than with this book (I could not have done it without him!); my friend, Justin Gould, for kindly allowing me to use several of his stunning photographs from his website www.sparks.com for which I am grateful; and, finally, Robin Messer, a great friend whose photography advice and assistance are very much appreciated.

A FIREFLY BOOK

Published by Firefly Books Ltd., 2002

Copyright © 2002 Martin Treasure

All rights reserved. No part of this publication may be reproduced, stored in a retrieval system or transmitted in any form or by any means, electronic, mechanical, photocopying, recording or otherwise, without the prior written permission of the publisher.

First Printing

**National Library of Canada
Cataloguing in Publication Data**
Treasure, Martin
     Bonsai life histories
Includes index.
ISBN 1-55209-617-3 (bound)   ISBN 1-55209-615-7 (pbk.)
1. Bonsai. I. Title.
SB433.5.T73 2001   635.9'772
C2001-930406-4

**U.S. Cataloging in Publication Data
(Library of Congress Standards)**
Bonsai life histories / David Treasure. – 1st ed.
[144] p. ; col. photos. : cm.
ISBN: 1-55209-617-3
ISBN: 1-55209-615-7 (pbk)
1. Bonsai. 2. Indoor bonsai. I. Title.
635.9772   21 CIP SB433.5.T77 2001

Photographs by Justin Gould on page 6, page 18 (top right), page 20 (bottom right), page 21 (bottom right), page 22 (top right), page 45 (top right background).

All other photographs by the author; all bonsai trees owned by the author.

Printed in Hong Kong

Published in Canada in 2002 by
Firefly Books Ltd.
3680 Victoria Park Avenue
Willowdale, Ontario M2H 3K1

Published in the United States in 2002 by
Firefly Books (U.S.) Inc.
P.O. Box 1338, Ellicott Station
Buffalo, New York 14205

contents

introduction

history

Bonsai trees are often thought to have originated from Japan, but records over 2,000 years old show trees being grown in China as part of landscapes planted in shallow containers. Around 1,500 years ago, trees were first grown as individual specimens, many of which would have been collected from mountainous regions, and these can be seen in ancient Chinese line drawings. Several centuries later, the Japanese began growing and training trees in pots and have developed the hobby to its current level of sophistication. Chinese and Japanese bonsai are very different, with Chinese-style trees being more freeform and trained mainly by pruning, while Japanese trees are meticulously groomed and shaped, appearing more natural.

the hobby

The growing of bonsai, which literally translates as "plant in a tray," is a truly satisfying hobby and combines both horticulture and art, creating trees that are often referred to as "living sculptures." Above all, it is important that the trees are kept healthy and in excellent condition, as with any potted plant. Pruning and shaping does, however, require a degree of artistic imagination to visualize the future development of the trunk and branches.

Bonsai should embody all that is so wonderful about trees that naturally grow in such a variety of shapes and sizes. Large specimen trees, ancient trees with hollow trunks, trees that have been shaped by severe weather conditions or even small forests can all be recreated in the confines of a pot. By growing trees in this way, it is possible to have a mini arboretum of delightful, small trees in your own garden or even on a balcony, however limited in size.

The timescale to create impressive bonsai is dependent upon the origin, general health of the tree and the species. Trees grown from seed or cuttings will invariably take longer to attain the images required than much older material, perhaps collected from the wild or obtained as nursery stock. It can be most rewarding to build a collection from a variety of different sources. Actual age, however, is not as important as the illusion of how old the tree appears — a well-trained bonsai may look far older than it really is.

right: **Bonsai artists often take inspiration from nature. This ancient bristlecone pine has many attractive features that could be combined to good effect in a bonsai, especially to simulate juniper.**

misconceptions

A common misconception about the hobby is that it is cruel, with the trees being starved in order to dwarf them. Nothing could be further from the truth. Bonsai trees require regular watering, feeding and repotting to keep them in optimum health, and in many cases they are actually healthier than their counterparts in the wild, enjoying the same longevity. Some trees in Japan have recorded histories spanning several centuries and are often traditionally passed from generation to generation, keeping them in the same family during their long life-times. Root pruning is a widespread horticultural technique, used by many gardeners to produce better root systems on plants grown both in pots and in the garden, and is not just associated with bonsai train-ing. This practice facilitates the growth of a well-developed, compact root system with many fine, fibrous roots that are vital for taking up nutrients, and does not restrict the overall growth. Various branch- and shoot-pruning techniques are the methods by which the tree is dwarfed, in the same way as trimming a hedge keeps it from growing into a line of large trees.

indoor or outdoor?

Many species of tree and woody shrub are suitable for training as bonsai, but if planted in the garden they would grow into full-size specimens — there is no such thing as a special "bonsai species." Pruning and shaping are required to create and maintain the desired shape and size. Some trees are often used to achieve the appearance of different species; for example, a juniper can look very effective when trained in the image of a pine. Trees that would naturally grow out-doors must not be cultivated indoors, where they cannot flourish and will soon die. Occasionally, outdoor bonsai may be viewed in the house, provided that a cool area is selected and that the duration is no longer than a couple of days. Only tropical species of trees are suitable for growing indoors. Figs, serrissas and pomegranates make particu-larly good subjects, although even these can benefit from spending the summer months outside.

appreciating bonsai

Bonsai can quickly become an important and very enjoyable part of your life. Do not be afraid to experiment with material — it is all part of the learning curve. Spend time studying trees at exhibitions and in books to determine what makes them good or bad bonsai specimens. Most trees have faults of some kind and it is important to be able to identify these, but do look beyond individual features and learn to enjoy the actual bonsai tree as a whole unit.

Patience is a definite virtue and the process of creating bonsai trees should not be hurried unnecessarily. Good bonsai can be trained in a relatively short space of time, provided that suitable material is selected from the beginning. Some of my trees have not always started out as ideal material, but through perseverance, surprising and satisfying results have been achieved. This is illustrated in this book by prime examples of the many detailed histories of trees drawn from my personal collection of bonsai, which I have had the immense pleasure of growing for many years.

above: **Crassula is often grown as a succulent houseplant, but its woody stems and trunk make it a suitable species for training as an indoor bonsai. This specimen is extremely large and over the years many cuttings have been successfully rooted, one of which is pictured next to the parent tree.**

left: **Take time to notice exceptional features on trees growing naturally, such as the superb root flair on this large European beech. Bonsai certainly helps you appreciate the wonder of full-grown trees, although moss should not be allowed to cover a bonsai in this way.**

getting started

The choice of potential bonsai material is almost limitless and many suitable subjects can be obtained at minimal cost. When starting out in the hobby with newly acquired trees, however, it is natural to feel somewhat apprehensive about how to proceed. These feelings are soon replaced by excitement and satisfaction as you gain more experience and your confidence begins to grow, along with your trees.

bonsai sources

seed

Growing bonsai from seed is a very slow process, where much patience is required. There is no such thing as bonsai tree seeds. A bonsai seed kit simply contains a selection of tree seeds that would grow into large trees if planted in the ground. Also, these seeds are not always ideal species for bonsai. It is much better to purchase selected varieties individually, since then you will know what seedlings to expect. Seeds do not, however, always grow true to the parent plant, with different characteristics sometimes appearing.

Growing from seed is certainly very rewarding, since you have complete control of the seedling's training from the very beginning, with endless possibilities. The process can be considerably quicker by planting year-old seedlings in the garden, enabling the young trees to grow more rapidly and the trunks to thicken. Training can be initiated at this stage, with credible results being achieved in as little as four or five years, but be prepared to wait longer — you should look on this as being a long-term process. To avoid becoming disheartened and losing enthusiasm because of this slow approach, it is advisable to increase your collection by other means, as well.

left: **Grown from seed, this Amur maple (*Acer tataricum* ssp. *ginnala*) spent its first year growing in a flower pot, and after removing its tap root to encourage a shallow, more fibrous root system, it was planted in the open ground for three years. When dug up, all the branches were pruned off, with the height being reduced from 5ft (1.5m) to 8in (20cm). A similar proportion of roots was then removed.**

left: **At six years old, many branches were wired into position and a dense canopy of leaves soon developed on the well-tapered trunk. Further root pruning enabled planting in a more suitable, shallower pot.**

left: **This Monterey cypress was grown using seed from a typical bonsai kit. It took over four years to reach this stage and was not really a suitable variety for training as a bonsai. It has since been planted as part of a hedge and is now over 10ft (3m) high.**

cuttings

Cuttings have the advantage that they will always possess the same growth habit and characteristics as the parent plant. Therefore, if you are creating a group planting, deciduous trees will all leaf out at the same time and the leaves will be identical. There is the additional advantage that there will be no tap root and a good root system will be quick to establish.

Ideally, softwood cuttings should be taken in early summer and hardwood cuttings in autumn. If you have some prunings taken at the wrong time of the year, however, they may still root, so it is always worth a try.

Many species of deciduous and coniferous trees can be grown from cuttings, although some are much easier to root than others. Ideal subjects are maples, junipers, elms and many varieties of garden shrub. Pines are usually difficult, often not growing well on their own roots, and are normally grafted or grown from seed.

above: **Chinese elm (*Ulmus parvifolia*) is very easy to strike from cuttings and can be quick to train. This tree was rooted from a shoot trimmed off an existing Chinese elm bonsai. After just two years, the basic shape and structure was established. In less than five years, a very acceptable *shohin* bonsai has been created.**

left: **Nothing is easier to root than willow. Simply stand cuttings of any size in a bucket of water and roots will appear within a matter of weeks. Spring is the ideal time of year for best results.**

training tip

If you have stubborn cuttings of varieties other than willow, water them with the water in which willow cuttings have been rooted — it seems to contain magical rooting properties.

air layering

Air layering is an excellent way of increasing your bonsai collection and has many advantages. It is basically a very easy and successful method of taking giant cuttings and is best performed in late spring or early summer. The resulting trees will usually exhibit superb surface roots. You can be very selective with material, and if multiple-trunked bonsai are required, they can be rooted at the perfect point.

Although there are several procedures for carrying out air layering, my chosen method is to completely ring bark, that is, remove a ring of bark from the trunk. Choose a suitable branch — large branches can often be air layered with success. Remove a band of bark approximately 1in (2.5cm) wide from around the branch and paint with hormone rooting liquid. Remember that the roots will appear at the top of the cut, so plan the layering accordingly. Position a plastic bag around the cut and fill with sphagnum moss that has been soaked in water. Seal the top and bottom of the bag tightly around the branch with adhesive tape, to prevent the moss from drying out. If, however, watering does become necessary, make a small hole at the top of the bag through which water can be added, but also make several holes at the bottom to allow for drainage.

When the new, white roots appear inside the bag, wait until they begin to darken and mature. After this has happened, sever the branch just below the roots and carefully plant in peat or a similar potting medium. The roots should not be disturbed at this stage since they are very brittle.

The whole process, from initial ring barking to rooting and planting, may take as little as four to six weeks and is very rewarding. Extra protection is advised for trees propagated in this way (during their first winter.)

above: **An air-layered *Prunus* variety is pictured here several months after having been separated from the parent branch. The shoots have begun to extend, showing that the plant is well established. It took just six weeks to root adequately, although some species may take over a year.**

above: **Four and a half years later it is looking glorious and I am rewarded with many flowers every spring. If an air layer has not rooted before the onset of winter, it is important to protect it with an insulating material, such as bubblewrap or carpeting.**

bonsai nurseries

The obvious place to obtain bonsai trees is a bonsai nursery. Most sell trees at different stages in training, from raw material and field-grown stock to wonderful specimens that have been in training for many years. If you are looking for a particular species and can see only one or two for sale, ask if there are any more. Some nurseries display only a few of each kind and hide others away, ready to replenish stock when sold. Other nurseries display all their stock, providing a good selection to choose from.

Bonsai nurseries generally do not have the time to refine specimens and much imported stock is mass-produced and field-grown. Trees with potential are the bargains: those that with a few years' work can grow into true specimens. Field-grown stock is often a source of good material. Take time to assess the merits of the bonsai and avoid unhealthy trees.

bottom left: **This pomegranate (*Punica granatum*) was great value, mainly because it was straggly and in a dirty terra cotta pot. There were poor quality trees half the size nearby, but because they were in bonsai pots and had received minimal training, the price was more than double.**

below: **With two years' training this tree is looking very presentable and is well on the way to becoming a fine bonsai. You can make your mark on trees like this and they feel more like your own, rather than expensive specimen trees which require only general care and maintenance.**

collecting trees from the garden

One of the first places to look for potential bonsai material is actually in your own garden — an old juniper that has become too large, perhaps? Mature and woody shrubs that need replacing may be ideal subjects for bonsai training. Take a good look around friends' and neighbors' gardens as well. They may have a plant that catches your eye and might be happy to exchange it for a new shrub. Or it may be that several years down the line they decide to revamp their garden and remember that you were interested in a particular plant. This has happened to me several times.

The ideal time for collecting trees is early spring, although with good aftercare some can survive lifting at other, less ideal times of the year. When digging up trees, take time and care to retain as much of the original root system as possible. If the tree is large, it is advisable to remove some of the foliage. Deciduous trees can be cut back hard — by at least 50 percent, but more if the roots are poor — and will often bud back on the trunk. Conifers, however, should be pruned with more care, ensuring that a reasonable amount of foliage is retained for photosynthesis. Back budding can take place on some conifers after the tree is established.

training tip
Avoid the temptation to train too many trees at once. Otherwise, the ones that deserve the most attention will not get enough.

above: **Trees like this juniper and cryptomeria (rear) are a real find. My neighbor mentioned one day that he was going to change his front garden and remove the conifers from the center of his lawn. I managed to persuade him to hold off until the spring by offering to help dig them up and take them away. Both trees were over 20 years old with substantial trunks and an even arrangement of branches.**

left: **This azalea was dug up from a friend's garden. It had a very shallow and well-developed fibrous root system that enabled it to be repotted straight into a large bonsai pot. Most of the flower buds have been removed to allow the tree's energy to be channeled into new growth. If the foliage is growing well, you can be sure that the root system is doing likewise.**

above: **This cotoneaster had been dug up in a relative's garden six years ago in late spring. It was left lying bare-rooted on the ground for three days before I spotted it and saved its life, initially by standing the roots in water for several hours and then by planting it in a large flower pot.**

above: **After surviving its ordeal, it was many months before the tree began to grow with any vigor. The image has developed well and the bonsai is very seasonal, with small pink flowers in spring, rich green leaves in summer, and in autumn, berries followed by vivid red foliage.**

When establishing a tree that has been dug up, it is highly unlikely that the root system will be compact and shallow enough to allow potting straight into a small container, so do not be in a hurry to plant in a bonsai pot unless the root system really allows this. The most important consideration at this stage is to ensure that the tree will live and recover. Therefore, always use a container large enough to accommodate the root system without any major pruning. It may not always be practical, however, to plant straight into even a large pot or box, in which case the tree will often benefit from a year or two in the ground.

Even with good root systems, excellent aftercare is vital to enable the tree to survive. It should be replanted as soon as possible and kept in a sheltered, shaded area of the garden, with regular misting to ensure high levels of humidity. Training should not begin until the tree is well established. This usually takes at least two years and often longer.

right: **This well-trimmed beech hedge is full of potential bonsai. The many years of regular clipping have produced large, well-tapered trunks that are evenly branched. Often, hedges are removed as a garden changes, or the trees may have grown too large. In situations like this, be ready to assist so that you can be sure that the root systems are not ripped apart by eager, uncaring helpers.**

collecting trees from the wild

Before you even consider collecting trees from the wild, it is essential that you obtain permission from the landowner. Look especially for trees that are naturally dwarfed by growing in small pockets of soil or on top of a stone wall, or those that have been nibbled by animals such as deer or rabbits. Alternatively, larger trees can often be reduced considerably in height, and by growing a new leader, taper can be improved. Spring is an ideal time for collecting trees.

The many areas to look for potential bonsai material include fields, building sites and hedgerows, where they are being removed for the building of new roads. Be selective and choose trees with well-developed trunk lines and solid bases.

right: **Many trees have colonized this abandoned quarry, including silver birch, hawthorn, elm, common maple and oak, growing in a variety of shapes and sizes. It provides an ideal hunting ground for potential bonsai.**

above: **This large European beech (*Fagus sylvatica*) was too difficult to move. Instead, the trunk was pruned hard and a trench dug around the tree, with heavy roots being severed. The trench was filled with fine soil to encourage fibrous roots and the tree was successfully lifted the following year. Patience was rewarded by the tree establishing quickly. A very large, deep bonsai pot allowed most of the roots to be retained.**

above: **Growing in very boggy soil, this beech clump was struggling to survive. The roots were in poor condition and I prepared an area of the garden with much grit and peat. All the branches were pruned heavily to ensure that the roots were able to support the tree. It grew in the ground for the next three years and was then transplanted into a bonsai pot, where training could begin.**

garden center stock

Most garden centers contain a wide variety of trees and shrubs, many of which are suitable for training as bonsai. By regularly visiting different garden centers, you will probably be surprised at how often the stock changes. Always be on the lookout for that special tree with the potential to become a truly wonderful bonsai. This may be a specimen shrub or possibly a stock plant.

Even if the plant is not displayed as being for sale, do not be afraid to ask if you can strike a deal. It is worth checking and often the price is very reasonable. If you cannot find something in particular that you are searching for, ask if it can be ordered. Some garden centers will order plants and let you look at them before deciding whether you wish to purchase them.

When examining garden center stock, dig down into the pot with your fingers to check the base of the tree, since this will almost certainly not be visible. Discard if the base is poor or if the trunk has an ugly graft, which will probably get worse in time.

above: **These impressive looking yews (*Taxus baccata*) have great potential and are reasonably priced. They all look very healthy, have strong trunks, are well branched and will bud back strongly if pruned hard.**

above: **Garden centers sell many types of tree that are ideal for group plantings, especially hedging material. These common junipers (*Juniperus communis*) were purchased at a local nursery where they had all been grown from cuttings several years previously.**

above: **I was able to select a variety of trunk thicknesses and heights, to help create depth within the planting. The trees were first pruned and wired, left for a year and then assembled in a large box, where they were allowed to settle in.**

training tip
Avoid choosing species with yellow or golden foliage, since this often gives the impression of the tree being deficient. Variegated varieties tend to be rather too fancy to make good bonsai subjects.

what makes a good bonsai

A well-developed, rounded crown with delicate branches

Trunk has gradual taper, an interesting shape and smooth, pale bark, without any marks or ugly scars

Branches start at roughly one-third of trunk height

Surface treatment of different types of moss and sieved Japanese akadama clay creates a natural effect

Excellent branch structure and ramification

Healthy, rich green foliage changes to a stunning yellow-pink in the autumn

Strong buttress and realistic surface roots make the tree seem solid and stable

Pot complements the trunk color and is a suitable size and shape

above: **This Korean hornbeam (*Carpinus turczaninowii*) is a fine bonsai specimen and has many good features. Attention to detail over several years has resulted in a pleasing overall appearance.**

what to avoid

When purchasing a bonsai tree or potential material, if a number of trees are available, considerable time can be saved by choosing a tree that exhibits the fewest faults, but still has the potential to become a good bonsai. Small faults can become interesting features of a bonsai, helping to give individual character and interest. There are specific faults, however, that should be avoided in all cases, since they may prove difficult to correct. These include inverse taper of the trunk, ugly grafts, one-sided or non-existent surface roots and branches that are too thick. Inadequate branches can be improved with careful pruning and shaping, but only if they are well positioned in the first place. Bar branches that emerge at the same height from opposite sides of the trunk are undesirable, looking contrived and unnatural. The lowest branches should normally be the largest and grow to one side, rather than straight toward the front or back.

A poor branch structure can, with time, be regrown on most deciduous trees. This is likely to be a long-term process, but worth persevering with if the tree has other redeeming features, such as a good trunk line or well-developed surface roots. However, this is not really an option with most conifers, although these species do have the advantage of being evergreen and therefore some faults may be hidden by the foliage.

right top and bottom: **This deciduous Japanese holly (*Ilex serrata*) displays many faults. Pictured below six months later, some of these have been improved, but the tree will never become a satisfactory bonsai because it is poor material with little to commend it.**

original, poor bonsai

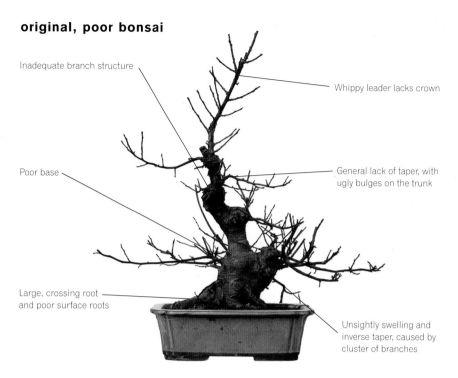

Inadequate branch structure

Whippy leader lacks crown

Poor base

General lack of taper, with ugly bulges on the trunk

Large, crossing root and poor surface roots

Unsightly swelling and inverse taper, caused by cluster of branches

six months later...

Leader thickening

Height reduced and crown improved

Branches structured, shortened where necessary and wired into new positions

Superfluous branches removed

More suitable pot — a good color to contrast with berries

bonsai styles

When styling and designing a bonsai, it is important to look closely at the tree and examine the different possibilities that present themselves. Decide first whether you are trying to create a young, old or ancient image and let the tree help you determine what your objectives should be. Remember that you are unlikely to achieve a convincingly aged-looking tree from a five-year-old sapling. Young trees in the wild tend to have upward-growing branches, while the branches of older trees will have been pulled downward over the years, as a result of the extra weight of their branches and foliage. In most cases the tree will help you choose the style, so you should avoid approaching the potential bonsai with fixed ideas. For example, you cannot create a formal upright bonsai from a tree with a curved trunk. Do bear in mind that bonsai rules are generally for guidance only and do not necessarily have to be strictly adhered to. Look to nature for inspiration, since bonsai styles have not been invented but actually recreate the ways in which different trees grow in their natural environments.

above: **A typical formal upright trunk and structure is evident on this cypress bonsai (*Chamaecyparis pisifera* 'Boulevard').**

above: **This redwood is a variant of the formal upright style and is one of the world's tallest trees, standing at over 360ft (110m) in height.**

formal upright – *Chokkan*

A completely straight, upright and well-tapered trunk with an even distribution of branches is necessary for this style. The first and main branch should be positioned at approximately one-third of the trunk's height. Subsequent branches should form a spiral pattern, becoming shorter and closer together nearer the apex of the tree, thus giving the bonsai a regular outline in the shape of a triangle. Well-developed surface roots help give the tree a convincing, stable look. Rectangular pots are normally used for this style.

This is one of the more difficult styles to create well and often appears somewhat contrived. Pines and conifers tend to be the most suitable material because of their natural tendency to grow in this form. The classic, formal, upright bonsai should be reminiscent of a strong specimen tree, where branches have been able to grow naturally with no restriction and perfection of form has been attained.

informal upright – *Moyogi*

Many bonsai can be placed within this category, and it is the most common style of tree both in bonsai and in nature, with the possibilities for design being endless. The trunk is not straight and may contain several curves, with branches usually emerging from the outside of these curves. This is a suitable style for all varieties of tree and shrub, and is perhaps the least difficult style to create. The apex will in most cases be directly above and in line with the base of the tree and for best effect be slightly angled forward to give the tree added depth. It is also a style where most shapes and colors of pot can be used, depending on the variety and size of the tree.

right: **Informal upright is a popular bonsai style, which is also widespread in nature, with many differing branch structures, illustrated here by a Korean hornbeam bonsai (*Carpinus turczaninowii*) and specimen English oak.**

literati – *Bunjingi*

This style was created by the scholars (*literati*) in ancient China and is often depicted by tall pines in old drawings and ink paintings. Literati trees frequently grow naturally in valleys or places where light has been restricted, resulting in a lack of lower branches.

A tall, slender trunk is necessary to create a graceful and elegant line. Although thought by many to be an easy style to create, a good, convincing and pleasing literati bonsai is often hard to achieve and potential material should be selected carefully. Shallow, round or primitive (rough and irregular), unglazed pots are preferable.

left: **Pines are often used to create the literati style. As this Scotch pine bonsai (*Pinus sylvestris*) shows, the style can be very natural in effect and inspiration can be taken from many different trees in nature.**

above: **The windswept juniper pictured here is growing on the coast and is a truly outstanding example of how bonsai can be inspired by nature.**

windswept – *Fukinagashi*

Heavily exposed to the strong elements of nature, this style creates a tree where virtually every single branch and twig has been forced to grow in one direction by strong prevailing winds. The trunk should slope heavily and strong surface roots are needed to give the bonsai the appearance of stability, even though the tree has been trained to grow to one side. Deadwood and jins are often created to further achieve the illusion of the struggle for survival that the tree has endured during its lifetime. In certain cases, trees that would otherwise be poor subjects for bonsai can be transformed when trained in this style, which must always create a feeling of great movement. Most types of pot are suitable, particularly primitive pots, crescent pots or slabs of natural rock.

cascade – *Kengai*

With its trunk growing in a downward direction and being planted in a deep pot (usually square or round) for stability, this style represents a tree growing on the side of a cliff or mountain. From this position in the wild, the tree reaches out for light and the trunk weakens. With the arrival of heavy snow and ice, or perhaps a landslide, together with its own branch weight, the trunk is bent downward. The base thus becomes the apex and the most vigorous part of the tree. In bonsai, regular thinning of the apex is therefore necessary to allow more energy to flow to the lower branches.

A cascade tree can be trained to allow optimum viewing from either the side or front, and the bonsai normally grows down beyond the base of the pot.

left: **This juniper bonsai (*Juniperus squamata* 'Blue Carpet') has been grown in the cascade style for many years and was trained from a small cutting —** *see* **pages 98–99 for the tree's case history.**

twin trunk – *Sokan*

Often referred to as the "mother and son" style, a second smaller trunk grows alongside the main tree. When styling, to give added depth, the secondary trunk should ideally be positioned slightly behind and not directly side by side, to avoid a flat, two-dimensional image. In classical twin trunks, the secondary trunk emerges at the base of the main tree, forming an acute angle. The first major branch normally grows on the smaller trunk. Pleasing variations can be achieved with the smaller trunk being either short or tall, and growing from slightly higher up the tree rather than from the base. Rectangular and oval pots are most suited to this style.

above: **Natural trees with two trunks are quite common, such as this elegant twin-trunk juniper, growing in Utah.**

left: **This large English elm bonsai (*Ulmus procera*) originated from a hedgerow and has a well-proportioned second trunk.**

root over rock – *Sekijoju*

The upper roots of the tree grip the rock tightly and are exposed by erosion over a period of years, so that they end up growing above soil level. Trees selected for this style should first be encouraged to grow long roots by planting in deep containers. When the roots have attained sufficient length and a suitable, interesting rock has been obtained, all soil is washed from them. The exposed roots are then tied tightly to the rock with soft string or raffia, following the grooves and contours where possible. At this stage the tree is planted in either a container large enough to accommodate the rock and allow the tree space to grow, or directly into the ground. Early spring is an ideal time for this procedure, when the tree is dormant. An alternative method uses several young saplings, each forming an individual root with the trunks bound tightly together above the rock, to form one tree — *see* pages 50–51 where this is illustrated in a case history. Trident maples are very suitable and are therefore most commonly used for this style, with the bonsai usually displayed in shallow oval or rectangular pots.

top left: **The roots of the trident maple bonsai (*Acer buergerianum*) pictured here were positioned over the rock seven years ago, when it was a two-year-old seedling.**

left: **Growing over rocky ground, the roots of this European beech have been uncovered by the effects of weathering.**

root on rock – *Ishitsuki*

This can be one or several trees planted directly on a rock, which then acts as the pot. The rock must contain a crevice or pocket large enough to retain the soil and roots of the bonsai. Trees can be grown on the top or side of the rock, depending on where the rock has the best planting positions. The

above: **These dwarf spruce (*see* pages 110–111) are planted on relatively soft tufa rock, allowing planting holes to be easily carved in selected positions.**

arrangement is best displayed in shallow pots with no drainage holes (*suibans*), filled with water. By using interesting rocks, it is possible to achieve a realistic scene of trees growing naturally on the top or sides of a sheer cliff or mountain.

right: **A lone juniper grows in a pocket of soil on the top of a cliff face.**

driftwood – *Sharimiki*

A large part of the tree will be deadwood in this style, with the remaining branches being supported by living, narrow strips that provide a lifeline. Trees can be collected with natural driftwood or the effect created by bark stripping and carving techniques. It is vital to leave one or more lifelines to transport sap to the living branches. The style can emulate a tree struck by lightning, or one ravaged by disease, strong winds, frost, snow or even where animals have eaten the bark. It can also be simulated by attaching a young, whippy sapling to a piece of driftwood, usually referred to as a "wrap-around" or *Tanuki*.

left: **The world's oldest tree is a bristlecone pine, over 4,600 years old, with the major part of the ancient tree being driftwood. This much younger bristlecone pine, growing nearby, is enduring the same harsh climate and exhibiting large driftwood areas.**

far left: **With an interesting driftwood feature, this needle juniper bonsai (*Juniperus rigida*) has been greatly improved over the years — *see* pages 96–97.**

group planting – *Yose-Ue*

In this style, separate trees, usually of one variety, are combined to create a natural-looking group. The trees do not need to be individual specimens in their own right. One-sided trees, which would be unsuitable for other styles, can be used and are often desirable, since branches in a group grow out toward the light and not into the center where light is excluded. Usually smaller, thinner trees are planted nearer the back and the outside, with larger, heavier-trunked trees at the front to create the desired perspective and feeling of distance. Young or old trees can be utilized to create different effects.

Small groups should not contain even numbers of trees, to avoid the arrangement looking unnatural. Convincing groups can be created very quickly by selecting suitable trees, such as hedging material, which is often sold bare-rooted in the autumn and is inexpensive. Large, shallow, oval or rectangular pots, slates or stone slabs can be used to good effect, to create the appearance of a natural landscape.

top right: **Assembled seven years ago from collected saplings, this bonsai group of European beech trees (*Fagus sylvatica*) is very realistic.**

right: **These horse chestnut trees are growing in the center of a field and look stunning each spring when they are covered in thousands of large, white flowers.**

broom – *Hokidachi*

This very natural style of tree, often found growing in parkland, resembles an upturned broom. The trunk should be straight with fine, twiggy branches. Deciduous trees are most suitable for this style, enabling the branch ramification to be appreciated without leaves in the tree's winter state. Branches should start from a point on the trunk about one-third of the total height of the tree. They usually emerge from one area, although this is not always the case and variants are possible. A good broom bonsai will take several years to develop the necessary fine branch structure. Zelkovas, elms and maples are ideal subjects and are shown to their best advantage in shallow oval or rectangular pots.

right: **The similarities between this *Zelkova serrata* bonsai and the wild sycamore tree are striking and both display a balanced arrangement of twiggy branches, with good straight trunks.**

other bonsai styles

Slanting Trunk leaning, with branches on both sides; apex to one side of the base

Semi-cascade Growing in a gentle downward and horizontal direction, but not below the base of the pot

Triple Trunk Tree with three trunks, usually originating at soil level

Clump Several trunks grow from the roots of one tree, creating a small woodland effect

Raft Tree lying on its side with branches growing from the trunk to form a group of trees

Weeping Informal upright tree with branches weeping vertically — usually willow, birch or tamarix

Candle Flame Upward-growing branches form a flame shape — typically associated with ginkgos

Two Tree Two separate trees planted close together, resembling a twin trunk

Octopus Multi-trunk variant with many twisted trunks — usually pines

Split Trunk Trunk has been literally split to form separate elements

Exposed Root Base of trunk is formed by heavy, woody, exposed roots

Twisted Trunk Trunk that appears to twist and spiral — often seen with pomegranates

Coiled Trunk Grotesque, with severe bends in the trunk

Landscape Group of trees planted with rocks to form a realistic miniature landscape

top styling tips

• In most styles, positioning the apex of the tree directly over the base makes the bonsai appear well balanced.

• To add depth and perspective, the top/apex should lean slightly forward in most styles other than formal uprights.

• The ends of branches should be level with the soil, rather than pointing upward or downward, to create the appearance of stability.

• Work toward triangular outlines for most styles, with larger branches lower down.

• Main branches should be welcoming, in the way that you might greet someone with your arms.

care and training

T he creation of a good bonsai is achieved by a combination of care and training, with both aspects being of equal importance. Care is the horticultural element, determining the health and general well-being of the tree, while training is the artistic side, responsible for achieving the shape and overall form. Together, these two areas combine to create the final image and appearance of the bonsai.

Watering and feeding are the most fundamental of all the requirements, to ensure that your bonsai grows well. It is vital that the tree is not only alive but happy and healthy, being free from pests and diseases, before any pruning and training is initiated. A well-established root system and correct siting of the tree are also important factors.

watering

Growing in such small containers, with incredibly efficient root systems and often dense canopies of foliage, it is hardly surprising that bonsai trees require regular watering as they grow. It is impossible to specify how often a bonsai will need to be watered, because there are so many underlying factors that should be taken into account. These include the weather, time of year, where the tree is situated, soil mix, depth of pot and the species. Some trees, such as pines, will tolerate drier conditions far better than others, such as thirsty willows.

Early in spring, as bonsai begin to awaken from their dormancy, it is time to think about how regularly you intend to water your trees as the seasons progress. This will certainly be a factor when you prepare your soil mix for trees that require repotting. Soil with a high proportion of grit in the mix will obviously dry out faster, but grit is essential for good drainage. When potted in a gritty, free-draining soil, it is difficult to overwater a healthy bonsai tree. However, if the mix is too free-draining and likely to dry out quickly, problems will be encountered, so a happy medium must be determined.

left: **When spring arrives, this yew (*Taxus baccata*) begins to grow and therefore its water intake increases dramatically. This is especially the case in deciduous trees, since they suddenly develop a canopy of leaves that demand water.**

To some extent, trees can be "trained" at the beginning of spring to thrive on more or less water. If you water sparingly as the trees begin to grow, you can carry on doing so throughout the summer. Conversely, if you start the growing season by watering heavily, then this is how you should continue during the year. It would certainly not be wise to change this routine suddenly, since the tree will have become accustomed to its available intake. Also bear in mind that heavy watering tends to produce larger leaves and needles.

For most species, an ideal time to water is just as the soil is almost dry, but of course this is not always practical or possible. During the summer, a good routine is to water at the beginning of the day and then check the trees in the evening, watering if necessary. A dull, overcast day with strong winds can be equally as drying as a hot, sunny day. Even if there has been rain, it often does not penetrate the dense foliage and wet the soil adequately, so be sure to check routinely. By topdressing the top 1in (2.5cm) of the soil mix with Japanese akadama clay, trees that are beginning to dry out can be easily spotted — the particles change color dramatically according to the moisture content.

If a tree does dry out, considerable damage can quickly result. This may not be fatal to the bonsai, but whole branches can die and the overall image may take years to recover to its former glory, if at all. Bear in mind that deciduous trees in leaf quickly show if they are stressed, by wilting. This state usually indicates that the tree is dry and urgently needs watering, although it may be a sign of waterlogging, as a result of root rot (see Diseases, page 43). However, a dry juniper will not look as though it is suffering and it may be several weeks until you are aware of the resulting damage, by which time it will probably be too late to rescue it. For example, a spruce Christmas tree brought into the house without roots remains green for several weeks before its demise becomes apparent.

Watering with collected rain water is ideal, but tap water is perfectly acceptable in most cases. Wet the soil thoroughly so that water runs from the drainage holes, washing away any salts and deposits that may have built up at the bottom of the pot. Bonsai trees can be watered at any time of the day, but when in full sun, avoid splashing the foliage since this can sometimes cause scorching. In winter trees will benefit from shelter from rain and frost. Trees can still dry out at this time of year, however, so check regularly. In cold, frosty weather, it is difficult to water a tree when soil is frozen. Water in the morning so that the soil is not saturated should it become frosty during the night.

feeding

Growing in such a small amount of soil, it is easy for a bonsai tree to become deficient when not fertilized adequately. Contrary to popular belief, bonsai are certainly not starved to keep them dwarfed. When to feed, what kind and how much fertilizer to use all depend on the growth that is required. A young tree may need heavy feeding so that it grows vigorously; therefore, a fertilizer with a high-nitrogen content should be selected. However, a mature, well-developed, deciduous bonsai should be fed sparingly so that the fine tracery of twigs does not become thick and clumsy. You can control exactly how your tree grows by correct feeding.

Fertilizers contain three main elements, known as NPK: nitrogen (for foliage), phosphorus (for roots) and potassium (for flowers). Therefore, a fertilizer with an NPK ratio of 10:5:5 has a high-nitrogen content and will promote strong growth. To encourage flowering, use feeds high in potash, such as bone meal, which can be sprinkled on the soil in the autumn. To harden off new growth in preparation for the winter, reduce the nitrogen content toward the end of the summer, switching to a feed such as tomato fertilizer and subsequently to a specialist bonsai fertilizer with an NPK ratio of 0:10:10, which contains no nitrogen.

Liquid feeding has the advantage that it can quickly improve the appearance of a yellowing, deficient tree. Never exceed the dose stated on the package, but instead always mix slightly weaker than the recommended dosage — a half to three-quarters strength is ideal and will make sure that the roots are never scorched. Feeding weaker solutions little and often is far better than giving occasional strong feeds. Before feeding the trees, take time to water them thoroughly so that all the fertilizer can be fully absorbed. Do not liquid feed on days of heavy rain, because the fertilizer may be washed out of the soil before the trees can benefit.

Slow-release fertilizers specially formulated for bonsai are invaluable and can be used in addition to liquid feeds. These come in many different shapes and sizes, such as rapeseed cakes, pellets, granules and powder. The growth of each individual tree can easily be regulated by adding more or fewer pellets to the soil surface. A large tree may only need a few pellets to keep it healthy, but many more to make it grow with vigor. Often after several days the pellets develop a mold, which is quite normal and shows that they are beginning to break down and feed the tree, lasting for several weeks. I have also used chicken manure in pellet form with good results, which is inexpensive and readily available at most garden centers.

Only trees that have healthy, established root systems should be fed. For freshly repotted trees, begin fertilizing using weak liquid feeds at least one month after root pruning has been undertaken. When repotting trees, it is a good idea to add a small amount of slow-release fertilizer granules to the soil mix. These will activate and provide a basic feed as the soil temperature rises, although supplementing with other feeds may be required later on.

Using more than one fertilizer brand and type during the growing season will help to ensure that a good balance of nutrients is available to the tree. Foliar feeds, which involve misting the foliage with a solution of fertilizer, offer an excellent way of keeping the tree healthy without encouraging growth.

site selection

Most species of bonsai can quite happily tolerate full sun and will thrive in this situation. A bright position is essential for good budding and healthy, compact growth. If kept in a shady area, the leaves can become larger with shoots, quickly growing leggy and sparse. It is important to realize that bonsai soon become accustomed to their environment, and with this in mind, they should be sited in late spring where they will remain for the summer. Hornbeams and maples are often mistakenly believed to be shade lovers. In fact, they will grow happily and strongly in full sunlight. If grown in heavy shade, however, and then suddenly moved into a position where they will receive strong sunlight, scorching of the leaves is an almost inevitable consequence.

Most of my bonsai are sited where they receive maximum light, with the exception of zelkovas and willows. I have found through experience that these species prefer slight shade and grow better when kept out of strong sun.

Bonsai trees are best viewed at eye level and should be well spaced so that their structure and form can be easily appreciated. Keeping them off the ground also helps to deter some pests, and not over-crowding them allows optimum conditions for growth. Rotate the trees regularly so that the back and sides benefit from an equal amount of light. It is easy to enjoy a tree from the front without realizing that the back is suffering and beginning to die back through lack of light. The foliage of trees growing in good light will often be lighter in color to that of trees growing in heavy shade, because the leaves are working so efficiently. When positioned in shade, the foliage turns darker to absorb more sunlight. This is useful when preparing trees for exhibition, since by placing the chosen bonsai in shade for a few days, the leaves or needles will often become a much richer green color. However, this does not apply to trees with copper-colored leaves, which start to turn green if positioned in shade.

During winter and early spring, ensure that tender and finely branched trees are given adequate protection in a cold, well-ventilated greenhouse or a similar environment. They do not like the action of constant freezing and thawing. Any trees that show signs of being waterlogged should also be positioned out of rain or snow.

above: **I developed this hollow-trunk hawthorn (*Crataegus monogyna*) from collected material. The second trunk was removed to expose a concave area of the trunk, which I then made deeper by carving, resulting in the creation of an interesting deadwood feature.**

above: **Using a combination of liquid and slow-release fertilizers has resulted in lush, strong growth. The branches are being allowed to become overgrown to help them thicken, since they currently look too thin in relation to the heavy trunk.**

pruning, trimming and pinching

During late spring and throughout the summer, bonsai trees can quickly become overgrown, losing their shape and overall structure. The speed at which they grow depends on many factors, such as age, species and also the watering and feeding regime. To keep the growth balanced and in shape, pruning is necessary, and this is without doubt one of the most enjoyable and satisfying aspects of the hobby. Do not be afraid of pruning — it is an essential part of the development and maintenance of bonsai, helping to create miniature trees rather than overgrown bushes. Pruning can be an effective learning exercise, and if a mistake is made, there is a good chance that new growth will rectify the situation.

pruning

Deciduous trees usually grow far more rapidly than evergreen conifers, with new shoots extending quickly. Pruning them in late winter or early spring enables their form to be clearly seen. Make sure, however, you are aware of any branches that have died, to avoid removing a live branch and unwittingly leaving a dead one! Trees that have been winter-pruned will benefit from protection from the elements.

If possible when pruning, leave the bud at the end of the shoot pointing in the direction in which you require the growth to extend. This useful technique, known as "directional pruning," reduces the need for wiring.

When removing large branches, always ensure that the resulting wound is concave, so that it will heal neatly and quickly, and seal with wound sealant (available in a tube). An ideal time to remove large branches is during midsummer, after the initial burst of spring energy has subsided. This produces a smaller callus and less bleeding, although branches can usually be safely removed at most times of the year. In the case of conifers, consider the option of creating a jin. If you are unsure whether or not a branch should be removed completely, prune back hard first, leaving some buds that could regrow if desired.

left: **Pruning and trimming encourage branches to become more twiggy and also to bud back on older wood.**

Do not prune just to maintain a silhouette. The interior of the tree will quickly begin to die if it does not receive adequate light and ventilation. Lack of light and air flow can also encourage pests and diseases. Thin out dense areas of foliage to ensure that whole branches remain healthy. Leaf pruning deciduous trees can help considerably, preventing die-back (*see* opposite).

The top of the tree is the most vigorous area in nearly all species, with the lowest branches being weaker (azaleas and Kiyohime maples [*Acer palmatum* 'Kiyohime'] are notable exceptions to this growth pattern). This should always be taken into account when pruning or trimming trees. Therefore, it is usually necessary to prune harder higher up the tree. If a bonsai is left to grow unchecked, the top will quickly become dominant, with the fine shoots near the apex growing thick and out of scale.

trimming

Trees should be allowed periods of free growth to keep them healthy. There is a close relationship between new shoots and new roots. You can be sure that when a tree's shoots are extending, so are the roots. The extent of growth allowed will depend on the stage of training. A tree in the development stage will benefit greatly from a period of free growth, which will help to thicken up the branches and trunk. In the case of mature bonsai, growth should be kept more balanced; therefore, shoots need to be scissor-trimmed, pruning particularly vigorous shoots harder before they begin to sap strength from other areas of the tree. The result will be shorter internodal lengths and more compact growth. If a branch is weak, however, allow it to extend to provide it with extra strength.

pinching

Once a twiggy structure has become established, summer pinching is a useful technique to maintain the tree's shape and to develop greater ramification. For juniper, cypress, spruce, cryptomeria, larch and other similar conifers, hold the foliage in one hand and "pluck" the new growth. The shoots will be removed cleanly, while using scissors would cause more browning at the ends, especially in dry and sunny weather. With deciduous trees, such as maples, zelkovas, elms, beech and similar species, pinch out the growing tip once new shoots begin to unfurl and extend past the first set of leaves.

Pinching the candles on pine trees once they are fully extended will result in back budding and compact growth. It is worth taking out the dominant central shoot, to allow more strength to be channeled into the weaker side shoots. If the candles are allowed to develop into shoots, the size and strength of the tree will be increased. These shoots should then be cut to the required length in midsummer, or have the end buds removed to encourage denser growth the following year. Removing all the candles in spring as they start to extend will produce new buds both at the tip and further back. Some of these buds will open in the same year, producing compact growth with smaller needles. By using these techniques, and also controlling watering and feeding while the needles are opening, their length can be considerably reduced. Do not, however, aim for tiny spruce-like needles, since these look unnatural and can make the tree weak.

below: **When pinching candles, new growth or trimming shoots that make up a pad of foliage, prune harder on the outer areas and less in the center, to encourage a domed shape.**

training tip
When styling, regularly refer to the front of the tree to avoid making any hasty pruning decisions.

leaf pruning

The main reasons for leaf pruning deciduous bonsai trees are to produce a smaller crop of new leaves, to let light reach the inner and lower branches and to gain an extra year's growth. With a second flush of new leaves, the autumn color is also improved. Next year's buds will be activated and therefore the development of the bonsai is rapidly speeded up. Damaged or scorched leaves can be replaced with fresh new leaves, weak areas of branches can receive more light and ventilation, and spring can be enjoyed all over again.

The principle behind this effective technique is to encourage a new set of leaves after the spring leaves have hardened off and become "leathery." The bonsai is still strong enough to leaf out again, but lacks the initial burst of spring energy to produce large leaves. When dormant buds are activated, smaller leaves result. Only healthy trees that have previously been well fed and are growing strongly should ever receive this treatment. Any feeding, however, should be stopped two to three weeks before initiating this procedure, so that large leaves do not reappear.

If a tree does not re-leaf, do not despair. Leaves will probably reappear in spring, but do not leaf prune the next year. Failure to re-leaf can be caused by the tree being initially too weak at the time of defoliation, the removal of the leaves may have been too late in the year or the tree may not have received adequate sunlight afterwards.

Partial defoliation is another version of this technique. Large, outer leaves are removed, and in vigorous areas such as the top, foliage masses can be greatly thinned. Zelkovas respond particularly well to this treatment and it can be repeated again several weeks later if necessary, providing the tree has fully recovered.

above: **This air-layered Japanese mountain maple (*Acer palmatum*) is growing strongly. Early summer is an ideal time for leaf pruning.**

above: **One hour later, all the leaves and growing tips had been removed. Within six weeks the maple had grown a whole new set of smaller leaves.**

leaf pruning guidelines

• Correct timing is a vital factor — early summer is ideal. Do not leaf-prune after this time or the tree may not re-leaf.

• Cut off leaves so that the leaf stalk is left behind. These will fall off as the new buds at the base begin to swell and grow.

• Zelkovas have no leaf stalk and these are the only trees where leaves can be carefully pulled off by hand. Do not pull leaves from any other species, since it is likely that the leaf stalk will also be removed, together with the dormant bud that needs to be activated.

• Normally, all leaves should be removed, although foliage can be left on weaker branches that require extra strength. With the rest of the tree being bare, these remaining leaves draw the tree's energy into the branch and weak areas will quickly respond.

• Always remove growing tips; otherwise, the shoot will continue to extend and the desired back budding may not occur.

• When the tree has been leaf-pruned, its demand for water will drop, so water accordingly.

• Once leaf-pruned, the tree should be positioned in full sun for at least the first few weeks. This will encourage strong budding.

• Leaf-prune only strong, healthy trees. If a tree has been defoliated for several years consecutively, it will benefit from not being leaf pruned for a year.

• Leaf-prune only once a year. Defoliation is a demanding technique and the tree will need time to fully recover.

• Most trees should again be in full leaf sometime between four to six weeks after leaf pruning.

above: **The lower right-hand branch of this elegant European hornbeam (*Carpinus betulus*) was weak in comparison to the rest of the bonsai. With this in mind, all other areas of the tree were leaf pruned so that this branch would gain energy and strength. The bonsai originated from a bundle of hedging material and is pictured here six weeks after leaf pruning.**

training tip

Flowers and fruit remain the same size as a naturally growing tree and cannot be reduced, so be selective when choosing species for training as bonsai, opting for trees and shrubs that produce small flowers and berries. Trees with big flowers and fruit will appear more in scale when grown as larger bonsai.

wiring

There are many techniques for positioning branches, such as tying, hanging weights from them, using clamps and directional pruning (grow and clip — *see* page 27), but by far the easiest and most effective way to do this precisely is by wiring them. It is one of the most important styling techniques and with patience can be quickly mastered. Copper wire and aluminum bonsai wire are the two choices available and both can produce excellent results. Aluminum wire tends to be easier to bend and apply; therefore, thicker gauges are necessary for heavy branches. Anodized aluminum wire is very popular, being brown in color and therefore inconspicuous when applied neatly. Copper wire that has been softened by annealing strengthens as it is bent and is more difficult to wind around branches, but does have the advantage that thinner gauges can be used. Never use copper wire on *Prunus* varieties, since this species reacts badly to copper.

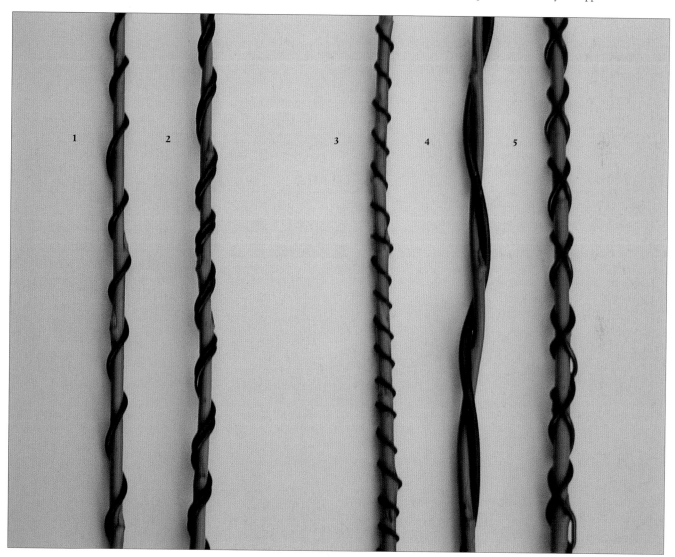

1 Perfect, well-spaced 45-degree wiring — this aluminum wire will be effective when bending the branch.
2 For extra strength, rather than using thick wire, neatly add another piece of wire.

3 The wiring is coiled far too closely and the wire used is too thin.
4 The wiring is coiled too far apart and the wire used is too thick.
5 Where two pieces of wire cross over like this, as the branch swells the sap flow will be stopped and the branch will suffer, eventually dying.

One of the most important aspects of wiring is to ensure that the wire is anchored securely before winding around the branch or trunk. If wiring two branches, use one length of wire for both so that they anchor each other. When wiring a trunk, carefully push the end of the wire into the soil to help hold it firmly. Take time to wire neatly and methodically at 45 degrees to the branch or trunk. This is the optimum spacing for best effect.

When wiring branches, make sure that the first bend in the wire is close to the trunk so that the branch is not torn or ripped away when being bent.

wiring guidelines

• Always apply the wire neatly and carefully — it will not only be tidier and less obvious, but more effective. Wiring that has been well executed can often be quite subtle and discreet.

• Use the correct gauge of wire so that the branch or trunk stays in the exact position right away and does not move. If unsure, test the flexibility of the tree first and compare it to the different gauges and thicknesses available.

• Never use wire that is too thick and difficult to apply. If the wire is not substantial enough to adequately bend, apply another wire of the same gauge parallel to the first wire — several times if necessary. This is much better than snapping or damaging branches as a result of struggling with unnecessarily thick wire.

• Branches can be twisted around so that the underside of the branch (or areas of the branch) can become the top side, as well as bent upward and downward.

• Wire may be left on for a period of between several weeks for very young shoots to over a year for thicker branches. As soon as the wire shows signs of biting into the bark, remove it so that it does not scar the bonsai. Small wire marks will soon disappear, but deep cuts can scar the tree forever. Replace if the branch moves from the desired position, keeping away from any previous wire marks.

• When removing wire, to avoid damaging the bonsai it is safest to cut it off completely, rather than attempting to unwind it.

• Wire the branches of deciduous trees in early spring, late fall or after leaf pruning, when the structure is much more visible.

• At some stage during a bonsai tree's development, it is highly beneficial to wire every single branch and twig so that they can be accurately placed where required. This can improve the appearance of the bonsai considerably and immediately. If this seems a rather onerous task, divide the time into sessions over several days.

• Support the area of branch or trunk being bent and bend slowly, gradually and carefully.

• When planning to bend branches, allow the tree to dry out so that they become less turgid and not so full of sap. This helps make the branches more flexible, but take care not to let the bonsai become too dry since this can damage the tree.

• Thick branches that are to be bent drastically should be wrapped with several layers of raffia for extra support. By wetting the raffia first, it is easier to bind more tightly.

• To bend a thick branch, hold it at the required angle as wire is applied around the branch. This helps the branch be repositioned more easily.

top left: **This Korean hornbeam (***Carpinus turczaninowii***) was developed quickly for sale and was probably grown in a field for several years early in its development. Despite this, it has an excellent tapering trunk line with no major cuts visible. However, the branches, although well distributed, were clumsy, growing at different angles and crossing in many places.**

top right: **After removing some unnecessary branches, both large and small, every single branch and twig was wired. These were then carefully positioned to create an elegant structure where the branches related to each other, with clean lines and good spacing between them. A shallower, more suitable pot was then chosen.**

left: **Five years later shows considerable improvement to the structure. The branch ramification has improved and the apex is now more rounded, giving this bonsai a fuller, more established appearance. Pictured here in winter, the tree retains its golden brown autumn leaves until the buds begin to swell in the spring.**

bonsai tools

Good bonsai tools play an important part in the maintenance and styling of trees. They are specifically designed for use on bonsai trees and it is worth investing in at least a few of the more essential ones when starting out in this hobby. It will certainly make working on your bonsai much easier and also help you achieve better results, rather than struggling with pruning shears, which can be clumsy. When used properly and looked after well, good tools will last for many years.

There are only a few tools that are truly essential, but it is useful to gradually build up a good, varied collection over the years, as you become more familiar with the different ways in which they can be used. It is important that you maintain your tools in good condition — clean and oil them regularly to prevent rust and keep them sharp at all times. Blunt tools can cause damage to a tree, while wounds that have been cleanly cut will heal far more quickly and effectively.

essential tool kit

1 Branch cutters/concave pruners The most important tool for any bonsai enthusiast, available in a wide range of sizes. These will easily prune off all but the thickest of branches with one cut, flush to the trunk if necessary, leaving a small, concave wound that will heal neatly.

2 Bonsai wire cutters Particularly useful for removing old wire from branches. The rounded tip enables wire to be cut from the branches without harming the tree, rather than unwinding the wire by hand.

3 Large scissors/shears A good pair of sturdy scissors that can be used for a variety of purposes, such as general shoot trimming and root pruning.

4 Long-handled scissors Excellent for pruning small branches, especially those that are in difficult to reach, twiggy areas of the tree.

5 "Snippers" Complete with a spring handle, ideal for easy leaf pruning and fine shoot trimming.

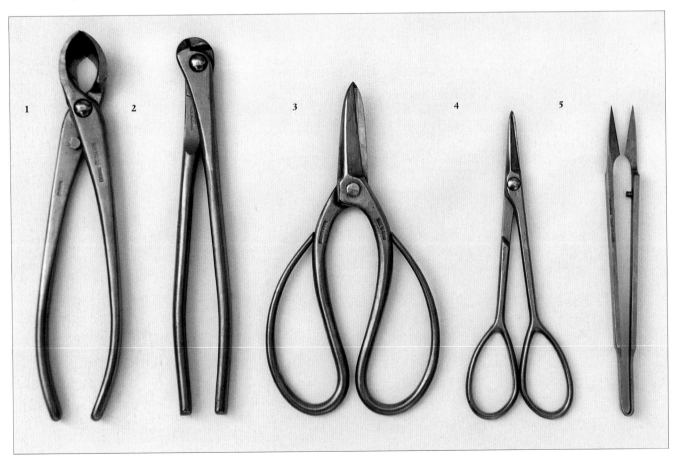

pruning and styling tools

Knob cutters Similar to branch cutters and designed to remove branch stubs, leaving an excellent spherical concave cut. This is a very handy tool. May be sold as "wen cutters."

Saw Finely toothed for removing heavy branches, trunk tops and large tap roots. Fold-up saws are invaluable on tree-collecting trips.

Clamps Used to bend or straighten thick branches and trunks. Apply extra cushioning at pressure points to prevent damage.

Tweezers For removing small buds, surface weeds and dead leaves among dense growth.

Small pliers Helpful when wiring branches, to bend the end of the wire; also to twist and tighten anchoring wires that secure the tree in the pot.

Bending levers A long handle enables thick, wired branches to be easily bent.

Turntable A must for any styling session, allowing the tree to be easily viewed from all angles. Use wedges or sand bags under the pot to change the trunk angle if required. Good turntables can be made from the base of office chairs or the swivel mechanism of a disused computer monitor. A large "Lazy Susan" would also work.

repotting tools

Chopsticks For carefully pushing the soil into any air pockets among the roots.

Sieves Different grades for sifting out large lumps from soil mixes or eliminating fine dust from Japanese akadama clay.

Toothbrush Good for cleaning algae from trunks and branches. Can also be used to expose surface roots.

Nylon-bristled scrubbing brush Useful for removing compacted top soil and brushing young surface roots outward from the trunk, helping to position them for the future. Also ideal for cleaning pots.

Heavy-duty root pruners Similar to branch cutters, but shaped like pincers and leaving a cut that is flat rather than concave. The long handles provide good leverage.

Bonsai fork or rake For combing out and removing soil from the outer roots.

Hook Another useful tool for combing out larger root balls.

Sharp knife Handy to cut down the sides of the root ball when removing potbound trees from their containers, especially when these are incurved.

carving tools

Chisels and carving tools For hollowing out deadwood areas and providing texture. Chisels can also be used to tidy up clumsy cuts to allow better healing.

Jinning pliers For gently crushing branches for jinning so that bark can be easily stripped. May also be used when tearing wood or branches to create a jin/deadwood area.

Chain saw Used in extreme circumstances to reduce the height of trees with thick trunks and also to initiate large carved areas.

Electric drills A large variety of cutting and sanding bits enable convincing carving of driftwood areas and jins. Take extreme care and wear goggles and a breathing mask. Protect the tree to avoid damage.

above: **This European beech (*Fagus sylvatica*) had a one-sided root system. An electric drill was used to drill two holes through the base to allow two beech saplings to be threaded through, providing new roots in the required area.**

right: **After three years of strong growth, the trunks had thickened and become part of the main tree. I then pruned off the tops of the saplings, leaving behind two small scars and two perfectly positioned new roots. The resulting base is now well balanced and the new roots are helping to support the tree, having become a living part of the beech.**

choosing pots

Bonsai pots come in a wide variety of shapes and sizes. When chosen carefully, a pot will help to transform and complete the overall image of the tree. Often, a developing bonsai tree may spend many years in a wide variety of training pots before being planted in its final container.

above: **A round drum pot suits the narrow, upright "candle flame" style of this ginkgo. The color is very subtle, being unglazed and earthy, and contrasts well with the bright autumn foliage. Two rows of studs help break up the depth and make the pot appear shallower.**

top right: **A large, oval pot of natural color complements this styrax, being deep to match the substantial trunk girth. A band halfway up splits the side into two smaller areas, lightening the depth. The flowing sides and spreading lip help to achieve a certain gracefulness, even though the pot is large. Being a flowering tree, a glazed pot would be equally suitable.**

right: **This graceful maple (*Acer palmatum*) is planted in a simple, light gray, oval pot, giving the tree an informal appearance. The pot has no lip and gently curved sides, enhancing the feminine appearance of the bonsai while remaining unobtrusive.**

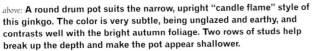

pot selection guidelines

• Never plant a tree in a bonsai pot if the roots will need to be drastically pruned in order to fit into the pot. If necessary, reduce the root ball and pot size gradually over a period of years.

• Bonsai pots must always have adequate drainage and be able to withstand freezing temperatures without breaking.

• The inside of a pot should be unglazed so that the roots can grip the interior firmly.

• As to exterior color, conifers are most suited to unglazed pots in natural browns and grays.

• Deciduous trees lend themselves to either unglazed or glazed pots of all colors, although subtle, subdued shades are usually most appropriate. Consider how the pot will blend with any strong autumn leaf colors.

• Flowering trees are often planted in glazed pots of brighter colors, such as blues, creams, greens and whites.

• If you are unsure what pot color to chose, select a shade to match that of the tree's trunk.

• Formally shaped trees look best in angular, straight-edged pots with sharp corners, usually rectangular.

• Less formal styles suit most shapes of pot, including rectangular with rounded corners, oval and round.

• Literati trees are usually potted in round pots, which can be primitive (rough and irregular) in design.

• Cascade and semi-cascade trees require deep pots, both for stability and visual balance.

• Group plantings should be potted in large, shallow pots or slabs of rock, allowing the appearance of a natural landscape to be created.

• Delicate trees can be matched with more fancy, dainty pots, which may have ornate feet.

• Usually, the length of a pot should be approximately two-thirds the height of a tree, or if it is a wide, spreading bonsai, two-thirds of the width. Tall, thin trees, however, may look better in smaller pots.

• The depth of a pot should be roughly the diameter of the trunk base. Therefore, deep pots suit trees with thick trunks, while slender-trunked trees or bonsai grown over a rock are best planted in shallower pots.

• Small trees can be planted in large pots to create a more landscaped feeling. Conversely, large trees can be effectively underpotted to appear more dominant and powerful.

• Pots can be made to appear shallower by visual tricks that break up the surface, thus deceiving the eye. Pot bands, inset rectangular outlines, studs and partial glazing all achieve this.

• Highly glazed pots will soften in color as time passes. This aging process can be sped up by actually wiping the glaze with a dark-staining scratch remover for wood or similar fine oil.

• The pot should harmonize and complement the characteristics of the tree, showing the bonsai off to its best advantage, rather than overpowering it.

root pruning and repotting

It is necessary to repot bonsai trees to ensure that they remain healthy and continue to grow well. Well-developed fibrous roots are essential for balanced, even growth, and these are produced through root pruning. With a compact root system, full of fine, fibrous roots, the bonsai will be able to take up the nutrients that are essential for its well-being. It is a misconception that root pruning is responsible for the dwarfing of bonsai trees, since this is achieved by branch-pruning techniques.

The frequency with which a bonsai needs to be repotted depends on species, age, size and how well the tree has been growing. Trees that are either young, vigorous or very small are normally repotted every year. Older, established bonsai may need to be repotted only once in five years, or longer. Also, deciduous trees require repotting more frequently than conifers such as pines and junipers. If you are unsure whether your bonsai requires root pruning, carefully remove the tree from its pot when dormant and examine the roots to see if it is pot-bound. The ideal time of the year for root pruning and repotting is early spring, just before or as soon as buds start to swell.

above: **This *Zelkova serrata* is around 12 years old and at this stage requires root pruning every year. The buds are beginning to swell as the tree emerges from dormancy, making it the perfect time to repot.**

tree history

Choosing pots one summer at a large bonsai nursery, I noticed a selection of over 50 small zelkovas. Most had the potential to become good broom-style bonsai and they were very reasonably priced, being planted in terra cotta flower pots. I decided that it was time my collection had a broom-style zelkova and began a selection process. After over an hour I had narrowed it down to just three, and eventually chose this delightful tree, mainly for its straight trunk and very natural branch structure.

I repotted for the first time the following spring and was dismayed to find poor, thick roots. There were very few fibrous roots and I spent a long time carefully removing all of the thick, ugly roots, retaining as much fibrous root as possible. A fine root system would be essential for this tree's development in the broom style, being directly reflected in the resulting canopy. Six years later this has clearly been achieved, as shown by the repotting sequence that features this tree.

1 First, take time to trim the tree, if necessary, tidying up any long and unwanted growth. Before repotting, it is wise to have kept the tree under cover for several weeks so that the soil is fairly dry. It is much easier and more pleasant for both you and the bonsai to repot when the soil is not soggy.

Bonsai trees are normally secured in the pot by wire, and if this is the case, the wire should be cut from underneath the pot. With a pot that curves inward, it may be necessary to use a sharp knife to cut around the edge of the root ball. This will enable the tree to be easily removed from the pot.

2 If the tree has started to become pot-bound, with long roots growing around the edges of the pot, then it is time for repotting.
Try to avoid allowing trees to remain pot-bound for several years. This can severely weaken the tree, because its capability to obtain nutrients will be reduced and water will find it difficult to penetrate the soil.

If there is still space for the roots to grow, carefully return the tree to its pot and examine it again next year.

3 Remove the soil from the surface roots with a scrubbing brush — nylon-bristled brushes are ideal. This task is often easier to do by returning the tree to the pot, using it to support the root mass. Brush firmly, radiating outward from the trunk, but take care not to damage the roots. This simple action can improve the arrangement of the surface roots and excellent results can be achieved over a period of a few years. Convincing and interesting surface roots are highly desirable, since they make the bonsai look more stable, realistic and natural.

4 Use an old toothbrush to remove soil and moss from areas close to the trunk. Spend time carefully exposing surface roots. You may notice a root that is ugly and unnecessary, and this should be removed, providing that there are sufficient roots nearby to support that area of the tree. Reposition roots where necessary, using wire pegs to hold them in place. When carrying out the repotting procedure, a large tray is useful to prevent the surrounding area becoming untidy.

5 To prepare the roots for pruning, use a bonsai fork to comb all soil and grit from the outermost roots. Standing the tree on a box or an upturned pot can make this process easier.

Comb out roots from underneath the mass, after first removing any old mesh or wire. The result should be that the roots will now hang freely, ready for pruning.

6 It is essential to use sharp scissors so that the roots are cut cleanly and not squashed. Prune about one-third of the roots and certainly no more than half. This ensures adequate room for new root growth when the tree is planted in the pot.

7   Cut several small wedges around the root base where possible. This enables fresh soil to be introduced into the heart of the root ball, keeping it healthy by preventing the root mass and old soil from becoming compacted.

8   The standard bonsai mix that I prefer consists of equal parts grit, Japanese akadama clay and a peat-based soil. A large sieve should be used to remove any lumps in the peat and a finer sieve for the akadama, which contains undesirable dust.

If the tree is in good health, add a small amount of slow-release fertilizer granules to the mix. These will gradually release nutrients into the soil for about six months as the temperature rises, and should be used in addition to other feeds applied during the growing season.

9   After first cleaning the pot well, cover the drainage holes with plastic mesh and fasten with wire loops. Prepare long wires for securing the tree and thread these through suitable holes in the bottom of the pot. Add a layer of grit for drainage, followed by a layer of the dry bonsai soil mix — the amount to use will vary depending on the depth of the pot.

10   Take time positioning the tree in the pot — any mistake at this stage will have to wait until next year to be rectified. Secure with the wire ties so that the tree sits firmly in the pot. Movement while the new roots develop can be very damaging and strong winds are capable of blowing an unsecured bonsai tree out of its pot when it is newly repotted.

11   Use a chopstick to push the soil into awkward places, ensuring that no air pockets are present. Tapping the pot also helps.

Top-dress with Japanese akadama clay. This has the advantage of being both attractive and also a useful dryness indicator, changing to a much lighter color as the soil begins to dry out.

12   Finally, thoroughly water the tree and position it out of the wind. Protect from hard frosts and wait for the buds to open!

right: **The zelkova is pictured here two months after repotting. Once a year in early summer the tree is partially leaf pruned, leaving only the small leaves on the inner branches to give these shoots extra strength and prevent die-back. Over the next few years the canopy will be allowed to slowly increase in size.**

pests and diseases

A severe outbreak of pests or disease can be incredibly damaging for a bonsai tree. They are unable to outgrow infestations and as a result, extensive die-back and even death of the tree can occur. However, being fairly small and manageable, bonsai are usually easy to treat. Healthy, strong trees are often most resistant, but all trees should be regularly inspected so that any problems can be eradicated quickly, before they become serious and damaging.

treating pests

This can be done either chemically or organically, and both methods can be extremely effective. When mixing insecticide solutions, always follow the manufacturer's instructions exactly. Too weak a solution and the insects will remain; too strong and the foliage may be damaged. If in any doubt, test on a small back branch first. Most pests can be eliminated by using either systemic insecticides, which are absorbed directly into the plant's system, or contact insecticides, which must actually come into contact with the pests. Always treat chemicals with respect and spray in dull, still, dry conditions, away from pets and garden ponds. Simply keeping your bonsai on stands off the ground helps prevent attacks of wood lice and also stops garden worms entering the soil.

pest	symptom	chemical solution	aorganic solution
Aphids (including greenfly and blackfly)	Buds and shoots look deformed and curled. A sticky sugary substance known as "honeydew" appears, attracting ants and causing unsightly sooty mold.	Most systemic insecticides are suitable. Try "plant pins" containing systemic insecticide, which when pushed into the soil are absorbed into the tree's system, preventing the need for spraying. Root aphids should also be sprayed with systemic insecticides if apparent when repotting.	Wash off with water spray (aphids do not climb back) and control with a spray solution of organic soft soap. Sprinkle lacewing larvae over the tree from mid-spring onward (average temperature must be at least 50°F/10°C) — one larva eats over 300 aphids. Encourage ladybugs by not using insecticides in the garden.
Red spider mite	Mottling of the foliage, which turns from yellow to brown and then falls. Conifers are most often attacked.	Systemic insecticides.	Control with a solution of organic soft soap, spraying under the leaves. When temperature is above 61°F (16°C), tap phytoseiulus, a tiny harmless mite, over the tree. Increase levels of humidity around the tree.
Scale insect	Yellowing and wilting of the leaves. Look for small, limpet-like shells, often with white fluffy undersides, which may be visible on the trunk, branches and leaves.	Systemic insecticides. For a small outbreak, paint shells directly with alcohol, such as methylated spirits.	Pick off by hand. When temperature is above 57°F (14°C), steinernema nematodes can be applied (use of nematodes not currently permissible in the USA).
Caterpillars	Foliage is eaten and caterpillars are usually visible. Act quickly if several caterpillars are present.	Contact or systemic insecticides.	Use an environmental caterpillar treatment that leaves no harmful residues, or simply remove by hand.
Vine weevil	Larvae eat and destroy the root system. When the tree starts wilting, the problem is usually very serious. Adults often leave U-shaped holes in leaves.	Prevention is the best way to control this "evil weevil." Mix specific soil insecticides into the soil when repotting or water soil with vine weevil insecticide containing imidachlopid. Both treatments last for six months.	Prevent infestation by applying insect barrier glue to bonsai bench legs to protect plants from climbing weevils. Apply heterohabditis nematodes in late spring and in early autumn (use soil thermometer to check that soil temperature is at least 54°F/12°C).

treating diseases

Diseases such as mildew and rusts can be treated with any one of a multitude of fungicides available at all good garden centers. Poor air circulation is often the cause and simply keeping the bonsai in a well-ventilated position and thinning the foliage helps to prevent many of these problems. Some trees are more susceptible than others — even trees of the same species. Infected leaves should be removed and disposed of. The application of an annual winter wash is good practice for deciduous trees and some conifers to rid the bonsai of any overwintering diseases. This also cleans the trunk and branches, removing algae and lichens.

Root rot can usually be prevented by simply using free-draining soil, composed of at least one-third grit. If leaves wilt and begin to wither when the tree is not dry, there is usually a problem with the roots. Carefully inspect the root system and remove all brown, rotten roots. Pot in a mixture of at least one-half grit and position in a shady area, misting regularly. Cover the whole tree with a plastic bag if possible, creating a humid micro environment. Remove the bag every few days to prevent mildew developing.

above: **Originally collected from the wild, this English oak (*Quercus robur*) showed tremendous potential.**

left: **After five years of training, it has become a fine *shohin* bonsai. The oak apples pictured are caused by a gall wasp. On such a small bonsai they should be removed before the tree is weakened.**

bonsai season planner

Spring is perhaps the most exciting time of the year for the bonsai enthusiast, when plans and dreams can be acted upon and enthusiasm is at its greatest. The trees come back to life with a burst of energy and promise. Buds open, and leaves and shoots emerge looking fresh and green. This is the busiest time of the year and there is much to be done.

- Repot trees — now is the perfect time to improve a tree's appearance by giving it that special pot.
- Protect freshly repotted and tender trees from winds, rain and frost.
- Lift trees that you previously earmarked for collecting last year and search for others.
- Check garden centers for the arrival of new stocks of trees and examine carefully before purchasing — especially the root and base structure.
- Dig up trees in your garden that you have been growing and pot up. Plant out new stock that will benefit from a period in the ground.
- Style potential material that has an established root system, protecting from frosts.
- Prune out any dead branches or twigs as they become apparent.
- Structural pruning can be carried out on most trees, but avoid large branch removal at this stage on Chinese elms (*Ulmus parvifolia*), which

will later callus badly, or on pines and spruce, since resin will bleed from the wound and stain the bark. Do not be alarmed by maples and birches bleeding — they will come to no harm. The bleeding can be prevented or reduced by root pruning at the same time.

- Start preparing selected trees that are to be exhibited later in the year by giving them extra protection and attention.
- Repot and prepare accent plants.
- Check for pests and diseases, especially greenfly, which can quickly attack new tender shoots and leaves.
- Update photographs and records, particularly where interesting changes will be made.
- Trees will require watering more frequently as the weather warms and the roots and foliage begin to grow rapidly. You can now look forward to summer.

Summer, with its lighter evenings and better weather, gives you more time to enjoy your trees. They should now be looking glorious with their full canopy of foliage. There are still many tasks, however, that need to be completed.

- Display trees to their best advantage in your garden. Select a prominent position for single trees, which can then be carefully studied individually. This may be in the house, but for no more than a couple of days.
- Check for pests and diseases. These can easily strike unnoticed and do considerable damage, especially caterpillars.
- Protect against vine weevil by using insect barrier glue on all legs of stands, in conjunction with organic nematodes or soil pesticides.
- Regularly feed with liquid fertilizers and also slow-release pellets specifically for bonsai. Older, more established trees should be fed less than younger bonsai, to encourage fine twiggy growth.
- Keep an eye on watering, since transpiration is now at its maximum. Wind can have as much drying effect as a full day's sun. Willows can be stood in a dish of water throughout the summer.
- Prune when necessary since wounds will now heal quickly. Be sure to use wound sealant. Leaf pruning can be carried out in early summer.

- Style and wire trees. Be sure to take "before" and "after" photographs.
- Any wire that is beginning to bite into bark should be removed, but replaced if necessary.
- Keep all weeds in check, removing them as soon as they appear.
- Take planned air layerings in early summer, semi-hardwood cuttings and also pot up new seedlings.
- Enjoy walks in potential bonsai hunting grounds where permission has been obtained, looking for suitable trees to collect in the spring.
- Treat driftwood and jinned branches with lime sulfur on a sunny day, to speed up the bleaching process and enable it to dry quickly.
- Let trees grow freely for a period, unless they are being prepared for exhibition.
- When on holiday, do make sure that you have a reliable friend or neighbor to care for your trees. Demonstrate exactly what the watering procedure should be. A trial run is a good idea.
- In late summer, switch to low-nitrogen fertilizers, such as those used for feeding tomato plants. This will help branches ripen and harden during autumn.

As the bonsai growing period begins to draw to an end, many deciduous trees now reward you with a blaze of intense color. These changes may only be short-lived, but they are dramatic and the colors can vary from year to year, according to seasonal weather. Late autumn will bring frosts that will encourage the trees into dormancy and will not be detrimental to their well-being, as long as they are not particularly severe.

• Ensure that trees are only fed with nitrogen-free fertilizers in the period before dormancy. A sprinkling of bone meal on the soil surface of all trees, particularly pines and flowering bonsai, will be beneficial.
• Take photographs of the trees so that their autumn colors are recorded in all their glory.
• Trunks and branches will begin to thicken dramatically, so be on the lookout for wire biting and disfiguring branches. Remove wire where necessary and replace if the branch moves from its required position.
• Prepare the greenhouse or other overwintering accommodation for any trees that will need protection during the winter months.
• Thin out pine needles to enable next year's buds that are now forming, to receive maximum light.

• Remove excessive berries and fruit from flowering bonsai, since these can put a strain on the tree's energy.
• Use a toothbrush to carefully brush moss and lichens from trunks and surface roots.
• Tidy up, weed and dispose of fallen leaves.
• Take hardwood cuttings.
• Collect seeds from trees and store safely. Sow those that need stratification during the winter.

above: **This *Zelkova serrata* provides me with year-round interest, as illustrated here by these four seasonal photographs of the tree. I am rewarded with fiery red autumn foliage every year.**

Winter can be a wonderful time of the year. With deciduous trees now devoid of foliage, their fine branch ramification and overall structure can be fully appreciated, evaluated and corrected where necessary. Although the weather may be cold, wet and frosty with dark evenings, there are still many tasks that you can carry out. These relate mainly to preparation for next year, when, I hope, your bonsai will become even better and more rewarding.

• Ensure that tender and finely branched trees are given adequate protection from the elements. They do not like the action of constant freezing and thawing.
• Any trees that are showing signs of being waterlogged should be positioned out of the rain.

• Check for drying out. The trees will need watering occasionally over winter and this should not be overlooked. Water at the beginning of the day, so that by nightfall the pot is not full of water, in case of a heavy overnight frost.

• Photograph winter images, especially if there is a snowfall. Do not be alarmed by snow, since it can help to insulate the roots and maintain a more even temperature.
• Spray trees with a winter wash to remove algae, lichens and overwintering diseases.
• Check with your favorite bonsai nursery when the newly imported stock will be arriving. Make a note to visit immediately so that you have the best selection and the pick of any bargains.
• Take advantage of the lack of leaves to prune, wire and style. Protect any trees that have pruning work carried out.
• Winter exhibitions are popular in Japan and this idea is becoming more widespread, so prepare any bonsai that you plan to exhibit.
• Choose a sunny day to clean and re-paint your bonsai display bench, ready for the next growing season.
• Purchase soil, grit, wire and new pots. Begin to plan your repotting strategy and which pots to use.
• Clean out your potting shed in anticipation of the spring activities and sharpen tools.
• Sift and mix soil so that you are fully prepared when it is time for repotting in the spring.

life histories

K eeping photographic records of a tree's development is a very satisfying part of growing bonsai. Since the improvement over time is often gradual, with the trees being regularly viewed, it can be surprising to see the amazing transformations that have occurred when referring back to earlier photographs.

thick-trunked trident maple

Acer buergerianum

In the early days of establishing my collection I had many more trees than I do now. This allowed me to experiment with techniques, and there were always plenty of branches to practice my wiring on. However, most of my trees were similar in size, with none having trunks of any real girth, and I longed for the day when I would own a bonsai with a large trunk. I realized that the overall structure and appearance of the tree were what made a good bonsai and that "size does not matter." Nevertheless, I still felt that my collection needed variety of size.

A few months later I was fortunate to find a selection of trident maples for sale. The one that caught my eye was not only the largest but needed the most work to improve it. I had decided at the outset of this hobby that on the few occasions when I would buy a bonsai tree, I would never purchase a "finished" specimen, only one with real potential that I could develop myself. I felt that this was just such a tree.

I returned home with the trident maple and immediately displayed it in a place of honor on my bonsai bench, where it dwarfed the rest of my trees. I decided to select a new front, offering a more attractive view of the trunk, with improved gradual taper. However, I was then faced with a dilemma, since the branch arrangement was poor from this angle, with many major branches at the

Summer Year 1: **I first decided to change the front of the tree, since another angle provided a much better trunk line, showing off the fine buttress. However, the branches were not positioned well.**

Summer Year 1: **Early summer was an ideal time for pruning. I removed many branches completely and the rest I cut back, leaving just a stub to resprout. The tree was then set in full sunlight.**

back of the tree. I could either compromise and keep the original, less attractive front and existing branch structure, or cut off all the branches and regrow them. After convincing myself that the branches were poorly arranged anyway and had been grown too quickly, making them very straight, I decided to remove all of them. By regrowing the

branches slowly, I would be able to develop a much more interesting branch structure, and I was confident that this would eventually achieve the best result.

I watched the trident closely for the next few weeks as the new buds and shoots began to appear all over the tree in every place that I had hoped they would, and more besides.

Feeding the tree heavily, I let it grow freely while I studied the trunk and began to decide its future image. Later in the year I purchased a large, rectangular pot at a bonsai convention, which I felt would suit the trident maple admirably.

Spring arrived and it was time to repot. The tree had an excellent root system and was beginning to get pot-bound. I needed to root-prune very hard to enable the tree to be positioned correctly in its new pot. When the tree began to grow I wired and structured the branches, leaving more than were necessary while I decided which branches would finally be needed.

Over the next three years the tree was repotted annually and several main branches were removed, making the overall image less cluttered. The trident maple was allowed to grow strongly during this period so that the branches would thicken, and was pruned hard each spring.

The tree had finally reached a stage where it needed to be completely wired. I did this during the winter when I could view its leafless structure more clearly. Having been thoroughly thinned out, every single branch and twig was wired and carefully positioned. It was a day's work, but the result was well worth the effort.

After being allowed to extend slowly during Year 9, the apex was then given some much needed shaping. Being the most vigorous part of the tree, I had always kept it pruned hard to direct more energy into the other branches. Consequently, the top of the tree is not overly heavy and a good crown is now beginning to develop, enhancing the overall winter structure.

The leaves are regularly thinned, allowing light to reach the inner shoots. This also makes the branches more interesting, being made up of lots of small areas of foliage, rather than one big mass of leaves.

The development of this fine trident maple has been slow and gradual. It has taken many years to reach its present structure, but my patience has certainly been rewarded.

training tips

• Trident and other maples are usually tolerant of heavy root pruning.

• With its fleshy root system, the trident maple requires good winter protection in a cold greenhouse or similar environment, which in turn allows winter pruning to take place.

• Do not be afraid to regrow branches on an established bonsai. When in leaf the structure will be camouflaged, but without leaves in winter unsightly branches become all too obvious.

Spring Year 2: **To improve the buttress further, I uncovered 1½in (4cm) more of magnificent trunk and root flare that had been hidden under the soil.**

Early Summer Year 3: **Each spring, growth was pruned back hard, gradually creating interestingly shaped branches that were thickening well.**

Summer Year 6: **As a result of the wiring done the previous winter, every aspect of the tree began to relate to each other, particularly the well-balanced foliage masses.**

Early Spring Year 10:
The ideal time for wiring is when the tree is without leaves. Every single twig was carefully arranged and evenly positioned to spread them out, allowing maximum light to reach all parts.

Summer Year 10:
Throughout summer this trident maple is repeatedly thinned out to prevent the foliage masses becoming too heavy and dense. It is also leaf pruned most years, which helps to develop its twiggy structure.

Style: Informal upright
Height: 31in (79cm)

root-over-rock trident maple

Acer buergerianum

While visiting a bonsai nursery one spring day I noticed a very large and impressive root-over-rock trident maple, which had recently been imported from Japan. I had never seen a bonsai tree growing over such a large rock. The roots were old and gnarled, gripping the rock tightly. I studied the tree for several minutes until I realized that all was not as it seemed. Some branches were fully in leaf, others only partially leafed and several were not in leaf at all. Even stranger was that the leaf sizes, shapes and colors varied from branch to branch. The bonsai was in fact several trees combined together to create the illusion of one tree. Without leaves the bonsai would be completely convincing as a single tree and was a truly magnificent specimen.

This alternative technique for creating root-over-rock trees using separate trees as roots greatly appealed to me. That summer I selected seven trident maple seedlings that had identical leaves in all aspects and I eagerly waited for spring to arrive. I remembered that I had found a very interesting rock several years previously and had always planned to plant a tree over it, but the opportunity had never arisen – until now.

Finally spring arrived and I set to work. The trident maple seedlings were two years old and very pliable. I spent a long time carefully positioning the trees around the rock, using the actual trunks to form the roots. The seedlings were then tied tightly to the rock with string, which would eventually rot away. I did not use wire because it would have cut into the trunks very quickly and scarred them. The trees were bound together with

training tip
When binding with raffia, always wet first since this makes it easier to bind tightly.

Early Spring Year 1: **Seven trident maple seedlings with identical leaf characteristics await planting on an interesting, hard rock.**

Late Summer Year 1: **Only months after planting over the rock, the trees had grown considerably. This helped the trunks thicken and start joining together.**

raffia just above the rock, to form one single trunk, and then my new potential bonsai was planted in a large bonsai pot with the rock showing its best side to the front.

During the summer the trees grew strongly and were fed regularly. In the autumn the leaves changed color together and appeared to be identical hues, so I was pleased that I had selected suitable seedlings.

One year after its creation I was happy that the project looked promising, but I now needed to accelerate the growth. The trees and rock were therefore planted in the garden, with the rock being below ground level. Some of the saplings had already begun to thicken and fuse together. One overall trunk was quickly beginning to form.

Remaining in the ground for the next four years, the trees continued to grow well and reached 6½ft (2m) in height. The only maintenance carried out at this stage was occasional pruning of the trunks and branches to create taper. I also mulched heavily each spring with rotted horse manure.

The trunks had now formed a definite unit and I was anxious for the trees and "roots" not to thicken any more so that the rock would still appear to be in proportion. I nervously dug up the tree in late winter not knowing what to expect. I had not seen the rock for over four years and was apprehensive

Late Summer Year 1: **To help the trunks follow the rock's contours and grooves, I wedged pieces of styrofoam under the string to hold them securely in place.**

Late Winter Year 6: **After four years in the ground, the trees had "fused" together to become one single trunk growing over a rock. The project was a success!**

as I carefully removed the soil from around the rock with a fork. I was pleasantly surprised at the convincing "roots" that had been created by the trees and washed the remaining soil from the roots with a hose to expose them better.

After much deliberation I decided to use the previous back of the trees as the front. The roots seemed more realistic from that angle and the rock still looked reasonable. Two of the trunks had not grown as well as the rest and remained separate, so these were carefully joined to the main trunk with screws to ensure a good, close contact. I reduced the height by over three-quarters and completely pruned off all heavy branches, leaving many fine shoots. The "tree" was planted in a large, oval pot and the thicker roots pruned hard, leaving plenty of fibrous roots. I wired the remaining small shoots and positioned them to create the branches of this one tree. At last, after over five years, a root-over-rock bonsai tree was beginning to emerge.

The tree leafed out well and began to look impressive. I let it grow freely for the first few months to help it recover and regain its strength, then pruned it to create a basic structure. I find it hard when looking at the bonsai to remember that it is actually made up of seven completely separate trees!

Summer Year 7: **These seven trees now have the appearance of just one single tree with an interesting trunk line. I have slowly exposed surface roots, and with some serious wiring, pruning and defoliation, good branch pads have been formed.**

Style: Root over rock
Height: 22in (56cm)

two hedgerow maples

Acer campestre

The following two hedgerow maples were both collected from a hedgerow that was being removed to make way for a new road. As it was early summer, the trees were in full leaf, and with the help of an excavator complete with obliging operator, the largest tree was successfully lifted with the root ball remaining almost intact. I was convinced that this robust-looking tree would hardly even notice being moved.

A small seedling that was growing to one side of the hedgerow maple was also rescued and, being considerably smaller, was much easier to dig up.

Both trees were planted in the ground right away so that they could begin to recover and establish. Additionally, this would promote strong growth and help the trunks quickly thicken, since they were lacking in sufficient taper.

small hedgerow maple

This hedgerow maple started life as a small seedling, probably just over two years old. It was planted in the garden, but I always intended it to be a much smaller bonsai than the other hedgerow maple. Having a good root system, this tree was growing well after only a matter of weeks. The trunk was pencil thin and needed to develop considerably.

I pruned off all branches and trimmed the growth at the top. Abundant buds then formed on the trunk and the subsequent branches were not pruned at all over the next two years. During this time it was fed well and watered in dry weather. The result was a shrubby tangle of branches with shoots emerging in all directions, and since these were well distributed, the trunk was starting to thicken nicely. The maple remained in the ground for a further year and I trimmed all the shoots regularly to slow the growth down, because the trunk was nearing the size that I wanted.

Most of the branches were pruned off the next spring (Year 3), and I was left with a small, powerful and interestingly shaped trunk. The small wounds would soon callus over and vanish as the bark grew over them. Digging up the tree I noticed some good surface roots at the base of the trunk. Directly above, there was a large root spoiling the arrangement. I pruned off this overpowering root, enabling the buttress to be better exposed. The heavy roots were pruned hard to encourage fibrous roots closer to the trunk and I planted the tree in a large, rectangular pot. It grew well that year and I removed several branches near the base to expose the lower trunk, making it appear more tree-like.

Winter Year 2: **After two years in the ground, the seedling had become overgrown with many long branches, all helping to thicken the trunk.**

Spring Year 3: **With branches removed and trunk line exposed, the hedgerow maple was planted. It began to look more like a tree than a sapling.**

Summer Year 3: **The tree was not pruned until it was definitely established and growing well. The lower branches were removed to expose more of the attractive trunk.**

Summer Year 5: **A smaller pot was used to reduce the size of the root ball. The tree was leaf pruned for the first time and the new leaves were considerably smaller.**

It remained in this pot for a further year and was then planted in a slightly smaller training pot the following year, while the branches slowly extended. I fed it sparingly to encourage twiggy growth and leaf-pruned each year. After this time I purchased a small, pinkish-gray pot with this bonsai in mind. By being so much more contained, the tree appeared larger and the unglazed area at the bottom of the pot was almost the exact color of the trunk. This pot could have been made for the tree.

Every year this hedgerow maple is always the last of my trees to leaf out. It is also one of the last to drop its leaves when, for a couple of weeks, I enjoy its magical buttercup-yellow autumn colors.

training tip
Allowing many branches to grow freely all over the trunk, then removing them, will help to thicken the trunk without leaving major pruning scars.

Spring Year 9: **The appearance of the hedgerow maple has been greatly improved by using a more suitable, smaller pot. The tree has also been turned slightly to give the trunk a better line.**

Style: Informal upright
Height: 12in (30cm)

large hedgerow maple

This tree was by far the larger of the two — around 8ft (2.5m) tall. The base was excellent and the tree had obviously been trimmed back for many years while growing in the hedge. The upper part of the trunk was poor, being very straight and thick. Having a good buttress, a front was easy to select. I reduced the tree in height to about 10in (26cm), using a suitable side branch to train as a new leader. Anxious not to disturb the roots, since the tree was in leaf, a big hole was dug and the hedgerow maple planted in the ground to grow. Being a sunny day, the tree had started wilting. I watered it well and in a few hours the leaves had perked up and by the next week the shoots had begun to extend. The tree was allowed to grow with no pruning so that it could recover and the new leader could start to thicken. I rubbed off many persistent buds that kept forming at the base and mulched with well-rotted horse manure.

The next year the new leader grew considerably. A small shoot was utilized as a replacement apex, with the existing leader becoming a back branch, left only to thicken the trunk below. The rest of the tree was kept trimmed while this "sacrifice" branch grew strongly and thickened. When it was removed later in the summer, the pruning scar was hidden at the back of the tree. Good taper had been created in the leader, which was now starting to increase in girth. Over the next two years, the same process was repeated. More sacrifice branches were allowed to grow, which were removed annually. The main shoots grew vigorously each year and were pruned back hard.

After four years in the ground, the upper portion of the tree merged well with the original stump and a solid-shaped trunk, with excellent taper, had been created. Now 5ft (1.5m) tall, it was pruned down before being lifted in late spring and all branches were removed, leaving just the trunk. I reduced the height and planted it in a large, rectangular bonsai pot. All thick roots were cut back to fibrous roots where possible, and buds soon erupted all over the trunk. I selected those best positioned to create the formal branch structure I had in mind. Later in the year, several shoots were cut back and wired downward.

The following year (Year 6) I repotted the maple and allowed it to grow virtually unchecked, helping to thicken the lower branches. Occasional trimming at the top of the tree was necessary, since branches higher up should remain thinner and not become clumsy. New shoots were regularly wired into position and I knew that it would not be long until this tree became a good specimen.

In winter of Year 10 the tree was radically structured and thinned out, and several large branches were removed. This opened out the tree when in leaf and prevented it from looking like a mass of leaves. Extensive wiring was carried out, and I decided to make a feature of the lower branches, which I kept fairly long and spreading.

This method of growing and cutting back has been enhanced by the use of sacrifice branches, which were selected to grow at the back of the tree to make the scars undetectable from the front. A substantial trunk has been created in a relatively short space of time. In several years, being a maple, these wounds will callus over well.

training tip
Remove major branches during the summer, when the sap flow has slowed down. This will help to produce smaller calluses and reduce any bleeding.

Spring Year 3: **Just two years in the ground, the top of the trunk has thickened considerably. A small branch has been wired up to take over as the new leader. The rear growth will eventually be removed.**

Spring Year 6: **Pruning and wiring the previous autumn initiated good structure. By cutting young branches back, they formed more interesting, natural shapes than if they had been grown too quickly.**

Late Summer Year 7: **The hedgerow maple's foliage is a rich green and very dense. The branches are extending well, particularly the lower left-hand branch, which was also starting to thicken.**

Winter Year 10: **After removing many small shoots from between the branches and wiring the remaining structure, a clearly defined image has emerged. A good crown completes the picture.**

Summer Year 11: **By exposing more of the surface roots, a solid buttress is now apparent, making the tree appear solid and stable in the pot. The spreading form of the branches gives the tree extra width.**

Style: Informal upright
Height: 22in (56cm)

parent japanese mountain maple

Acer palmatum

While on holiday one year, I noticed a poster advertising a local bonsai exhibition. My interest in this rewarding hobby was just beginning and I only had a handful of trees. Keen to see some "real" bonsai, I attended the show the next day and had the good fortune to meet a knowledgeable enthusiast who invited me to view his collection the following day. His trees were wonderful and since I was a complete novice at the time he was keen to encourage my interest. He very generously gave me several small trees. One of these gifts was a small maple cutting that he had just rooted, about 4in (10cm) in height. This was to be the first of many maples I now have in both my bonsai collection and my garden.

My friend's advice was to let the tree grow for several years so that the trunk would thicken. I did just that and each year potted it in a larger flower pot, feeding well. The maple soon began to grow vigorously and I resisted the strong temptation to plant it in a bonsai pot.

Four years later, after reading an article in a bonsai magazine about the benefits of growing bonsai in the garden, I planted this maple in the ground, where it soon reached over 5ft (1.5m) high. It was a very attractive feature of the garden, but it was getting too large and needed reducing in height. I thought that this maple could now yield some air layerings and so I set to work. It was the ideal time of year, being late spring, and after a couple of hours, ten branches had been carefully layered. As the weeks passed two of the smaller branches died, but the rest continued to grow and it was not long before I noticed roots appearing in the moss-filled bags. When many roots became visible, I potted all my new maples into separate flower pots. I was glad that I had not just simply pruned off these unwanted branches. Instead, I now had the satisfaction of successfully propagating maples using the air-layering technique for the first time.

The maple remained in the ground for a further two years. It was then lifted in early spring and pruned hard. I decided to utilize a thick side branch that had grown upward, developing it as a second trunk, and planted the tree in a rectangular bonsai pot. The surface roots were poor and one large, ugly root was removed, slightly improving the buttress. Buds opened all over the tree and the shoots extended. I fed it very lightly to prevent the twigs becoming thick and out of proportion.

Two years later I leaf-pruned for the first time and wired many of the developing branches in an upward direction. That autumn the leaves turned a stunning fiery red, almost glowing.

After growing in the pot for three years, a more suitable dark blue, oval pot was found that, being slightly larger and shallower, suited the tree better. I exposed more surface roots and removed several small branches that were no longer needed.

The maple is root pruned each spring and thinned out extensively, so that when the leaves open, the canopy is not dense but airy and graceful, as a maple should be. Most years it is defoliated and is beginning to develop a good winter image. With a fine tracery of small twigs now present, the maple is improving each year.

Summer Year 4: **By its fourth year, the maple was growing strongly in the large flower pot. It was then planted in the ground the following spring.**

Early Spring Year 9: **Dug up five years later, the maple was overgrown. Its branches had been tied together to prevent spreading.**

Early Spring Year 9: **Heavy pruning left just two shortened branches and several twigs. Many dormant buds were activated.**

Summer Year 11: **Before leaf pruning, the maple was fed well and left to grow freely. This thickened the thinner branches.**

Autumn Year 15: **By carefully teasing out, brushing and arranging surface roots each spring when repotting, the buttress has been greatly improved, but the maple needs no help to look stunning in autumn.**

Style: Informal upright
Height: 24in (61cm)

air-layered japanese mountain maples

Acer palmatum

T he following two trees were both air layered from the maple detailed in the previous history on pages 56–57. They illustrate how, by selective air layering, good bonsai can be created in a relatively short time, and how a choice of styles can be achieved according to the point where the air layer is taken. As the maples share the same "mother plant," they have identical leaf size, shape and growth pattern, although the styles are completely different. They have, however, both received the same training techniques and care.

triple-trunk air layer

Keen to propagate a multi-trunked maple, I chose an ideal branch that divided into three. I ringbarked directly underneath where the branches joined and completed the air-layering technique. When adequate roots had emerged five weeks later, the tree was planted in a flower pot and placed in a sheltered area of the garden out of strong sunlight. I carefully tied the trunks together with string so that they would grow more closely, and this was the only training carried out that year.

The triple-trunk maple was planted in a larger flower pot in the spring. A good buttress was developing and the surface roots were already excellent, as is so often the case with air-layered trees. Now that the tree was strong, I began feeding it heavily to encourage vigorous growth and help the trunks thicken. I allowed the main trunk to grow without pruning for a further year, and lightly trimmed the other trunks to ensure that they attained different girths.

In the autumn the tree was very overgrown and three thick trunks were now apparent. The best viewing angle was clear, with the smallest trunk being on the left-hand side and angled slightly forward and the middle-sized trunk more toward the back. This ensured good depth and perspective, rather than having the trunks all in a line. Unnecessary branches were removed and the trunks reduced in height by about a third, with slightly more reduction on the biggest

Early Summer Year 1: **Weeks after severing and potting the air layer, it began to grow. The tree was then set in a sunny situation, where it gained strength.**

trunk and less on the smallest. Suitable side branches were selected to become the new leaders, which improved the taper. I wired several of the main branches slightly downward, curving them up toward the end of the branches. In spring the maple was root pruned and planted into an oval bonsai pot.

Training for the next five years consisted of much pinching and pruning as the shoots extended. Every spring the tree was repotted and each time care was taken to expose more surface roots. Several roots were repositioned and secured in place using wire pegs shaped like staples. By now the tree was becoming quite imposing and had started to outgrow its pot. I selected a larger, shallower, dark gray, oval pot and planted the tree slightly to the right of center, to counterbalance the movement of the left-hand trunk. I then spent several hours thoroughly structuring and wiring every single branch. Some were removed to provide a more open appearance when in leaf and to allow individual branches to be seen.

The maple looked far more impressive and elegant, with the overall appearance now greatly improved. Older-looking bark has started to form on the lower trunks, helping them achieve an appearance of maturity.

opposite top left, Summer Year 6: **Pinching out the growing tips helped develop the density of the branches and prevented long, straight growth.**

opposite bottom left, Early Spring Year 9: **With some major pruning, wiring and shaping, a more defined image appeared. The new pot curves slightly outward and, being larger, creates a more landscaped look.**

Autumn Year 9: **With trunks of progressive thicknesses and heights, the image of three separate trunks has been achieved. Most of the maple's branches have been trained outward, as they would naturally grow, reaching for light.**

Style: Triple trunk
Height: 25in (63cm)

patio-grown air-layer maple

I never actually intended this second maple to become a bonsai at all. I had so many successful maple air layerings that I decided to grow this particular tree as an attractive patio plant. After two years establishing a good root system in a flower pot, I transplanted the maple into a deep, ceramic patio pot, and filled the bottom third with a layer of large styrofoam chunks to improve the drainage and reduce the amount of soil required. This had the added advantage of keeping the pot light for moving around the patio.

As the years progressed, constant trimming of any long growth resulted in a very bushy tree, with dense foliage. The shoots had slowly lengthened and the trunk had started to thicken considerably. After the maple had been in the pot for five years, I decided to improve the appearance with some minor pruning and wiring. Some shoots had started to grow very upright and these were bent in a more downward direction. The very top of the tree also needed repositioning, since it was growing to one side. It was wired more upright and thinned out. At this stage the maple did not have a definite front and was constantly turned to receive maximum light on all sides since it was growing near to a wall. It was very three-dimensional, with evenly distributed branches — the direct result of regular turning.

By now the tree was most attractive and a real feature of the patio. The growth began to slow down as the tree was starting to get pot-bound. It was nevertheless still very healthy and I continued pinching the shoots for a further year. That spring I felt that it was high time to root-prune the maple, and with much resistance from the tree, I managed to lift it from the slightly incurved pot. The root system was indeed pot-bound and in need of some fresh soil. Without leaves, I noticed what a pleasing shape the maple had formed and I started to consider the possibilities of training it as a bonsai rather than a shapely bush. I closely studied the tree from all angles, trying to decide which would be the most suitable front, but it presented several options. After much deliberation I selected the view that I considered would look the best. I root-pruned hard, removing thick roots and leaving the more important fibrous roots. The surface roots were reasonable, but were crossing in several places. Two were removed to improve the root flare and the tree was planted in a large, round bonsai pot. I removed many major branches and generally thinned out any cluttered, clumsy growth to ensure an open and delicate structure when in leaf. The height was reduced by a quarter, pruning down to a suitable side branch that was growing upward, and this became the new leader. Many of the branches were now wired and positioned.

Looking at this tree I find it particularly satisfying that such an interesting and natural image has been created with such little effort. I particularly like the branch structure, which appears so maple-like, graceful and spreading. With time the surface roots will improve, the trunk will develop more mature bark and the branch ramification will build up, all enhancing this already sound maple.

Summer Year 1: **Just four months old, this air layering was already years ahead of cuttings and seedlings of equal age.**

Summer Year 7: **Growing in a large patio pot, regular pinching and minor wiring created a pleasant bush of leaves.**

Early Spring Year 9: **Noticing its potential, I styled and planted it in a bonsai pot. Hard root pruning was now possible.**

Summer Year 9: **I have retained the spreading habit that the tree was allowed to develop while in the patio pot and the result is a natural-looking tree that could easily be found growing in the wild.**

Style: Informal upright
Height: 26in (66cm)

air-layered top-section maple

In most bonsai collections there are trees that, for one reason or another, are never going to make good specimens unless drastic measures are taken. A friend from my local bonsai society had just such a maple among his many trees. One day in late spring when visiting him, he explained that he had grown the top of this bonsai far too quickly. He planned on removing it completely so that the tree could be restyled as a rather unusual semi-cascade, which he had decided would be a definite improvement. The top of the tree had received over three years' training and it seemed a shame to discard it. So, he had just performed an air-layering procedure to allow the top, when rooted, to be removed and become another bonsai maple. At the time, I had no knowledge of this method of propagation and was most interested to hear what had been done and learn this technique for myself. To my surprise, he offered me the actual air layer, once it had produced sufficient roots to survive on its own.

Six weeks later my friend phoned to tell me that the air layer had been successful and it was the ideal time to remove the top. I arrived with a selection of deep bonsai pots that might be suitable for the maple. We severed the air layer and carefully unwrapped the plastic that enclosed the sphagnum moss and fresh new roots. The tree was then potted into peat with the moss still in place, taking care not to disturb the delicate, brittle new roots. To assist the tree while establishing, the trunk was tightly tied in the pot with string so that it could not move and damage the roots. I was delighted with my new tree. Although the roots were less than six weeks old, the tree itself was already almost four years old and looking quite presentable. The whole process had been amazingly easy and I looked forward to trying it out myself.

As the maple began to grow strongly, I started feeding it and allowed it to grow freely for the rest of the year. When I repotted the next spring, the pot was full of healthy, fibrous roots and I removed all traces of the moss. The surface roots were incredibly well spaced and looked natural, emerging just above the original cut. This was going to be a real feature of this tree. It remained in the pot for the rest of the year, where it received some light pruning and general maintenance. However, I was not enamored with the sharp trunk curve. It still looked rather artificial. The trunk was too thick to bend, but I was confident that if it was planted in the ground for a few years it would thicken and the angle would become less pronounced. That spring the maple was planted in my front garden, where over the next five years it grew into a fairly large tree of over 5ft (1.5m) in height, despite some hard pruning.

After this time in the ground, the tree was reduced in height and planted in a large patio pot, where it was kept trimmed for a further three years until planted back into a bonsai pot. The trunk was much thicker and, as a result of pruning and regrowing a leader, well tapered. More importantly, the strong curve was now less severe and appeared far more gentle. The surface roots were exposed and were quite breathtaking. I had forgotten quite how convincing they were. The bonsai was now ready for some serious training and attention.

It would have been easy to persevere with the existing maple bonsai, which could never have become a good specimen. Instead, by being bold and starting again, an exceptional maple has been created with excellent prospects for the future.

Late Spring Year 1: **The parent maple's very thick base and slender, heavily curved trunk looked contrived. Air layering the top seemed a good solution.**

Summer Year 2: **One year later, the top of the donor maple was growing well, supported by its own healthy root system.**

training tips
• Consider saving bonsai specimens with a poor lower trunk and creating another tree from the top or side branch with air layering.

• Air-layered trees produce exceptional surface roots, radiating evenly around the trunk, appearing at the top of the original cut.

Summer Year 5: **With the maple in the garden, I practiced air layering on the actual air layer itself. Over two years I propagated many trees in this way.**

Early Spring Year 11: **The maple grew well in this patio pot for three years and had a good selection of suitably placed branches.**

Summer Year 12: **The branches now provide a rounded outline and the foliage is regularly thinned to maintain a light, airy feel, ready for the spectacular fall colors.**

Style: Informal upright
Height: 24in (61cm)

mature berberis

Berberis thunbergii atropurpurea

I remember the day clearly. It was a scorching Sunday at the end of August and I was exhibiting some of my trees at a nearby garden center. A friend had promised to come along for support. She had often said that one day she would dig me up a huge berberis that was the centerpiece of her front lawn because the tree was just too big. I did not think for one moment that this was the day! She arrived and proudly handed me a sack containing the largest-trunked berberis that I had ever seen. The roots were poor and the foliage was wilting. She explained that every year the tree would grow up to almost 6½ft (2m) high and then she would cut it back hard in the spring. This procedure had been going on for 40 years, yielding the enormous trunk and wonderful old bark. I thanked her very much, but thought that there was little chance of it surviving.

I packed up my trees at the end of the day and headed home with the berberis in the car. Once home, I pruned off all the branches, leaving the powerful trunk bare. The roots were also pruned hard since they were badly damaged and torn — this berberis had been quite a project to dig up. There was very little root left, so I was able to pot the tree into a bucket. It was left in a shady place to recover, but showed no signs of life. I left the tree unprotected all winter since I was convinced that, if not dead already, it soon would be. The berberis was soaked, frozen, covered in snow and completely forgotten. Spring arrived and to my complete surprise the berberis began to bud and grew strongly throughout the summer.

Following its resurrection I hoped to plant the tree into a bonsai pot the next spring, and removed it from the bucket. The tap root caused a problem, however, being as large as the trunk itself and growing downward. I spent time carefully "nibbling" the root away to allow the tree to sit comfortably in the round bonsai pot that I had chosen, and the large wound was painted with wound sealant. I trimmed the branches to create a definite structure and front. The berberis was left to establish in a cold greenhouse for the next month. I was not going to leave it at the back of the garden this year.

Many shoots appeared and I let them establish well into the summer. I carefully allowed the soil to dry out, reducing the sap in the branches and making them more flexible so that they could safely be positioned with wire. During the next four years the berberis remained in the same pot, being repotted twice. The branches were not pruned and grew unchecked for the rest of the year to help them thicken.

By now the berberis had outgrown its pot and so I purchased a larger, rectangular, Japanese pot that was a perfect match, the soft, purple color that would blend with the foliage. Wanting to make the tree look its absolute best, I wired every branch and twig, which now being older wood were easier to bend. The next day the tree was planted in its new pot and the overall appearance was greatly improved.

Spring Year 2: **I inspected my trees to make sure that everything was well. I was absolutely amazed when I noticed the berberis had begun growing — not just one or two buds but covered in them.**

Summer Year 2: **I let the shoots develop. They grew strongly and when I began wiring them, I discovered that they were extremely brittle, being full of sap and not at all pliable. Many broke off at their base.**

Spring Year 3: **I had a large, round pot that would complement the trunk, but I had no intention of using it if the roots were not well established. Removing the berberis from the bucket, I found the soil was full of roots. The tree was growing very strongly and so deserved the new bonsai pot.**

Summer Year 3: **This time, rather than wiring all the branches, I tied some of them downward. This looked a little clumsy, but no branches snapped. The berberis was looking more convincing, rather like a very old oak tree. It stayed in this pot for two years, where it grew happily.**

Summer Year 9: **In its new pot with extra room for the roots, the berberis grew even more strongly. During its training I concentrated on the styling, foliage, trunk and roots, and completely forgot that it was a flowering bonsai. The tree reminded me in summer when, for the first time, bright yellow flowers emerged, followed by red berries in autumn.**

Style: Informal upright. Height: 21in (53cm).
Trunk diameter: 6¼in (16cm)

reclaimed birches

Land containing many silver birch trees was being cleared and I was fortunate enough to obtain permission to collect any trees that I desired. It was late winter and I arrived at the site well prepared with several plastic bags, trowel, knife, hand saw, pruning shears and damp newspaper. There were many silver birch, but most of them were mere seedlings and not what I had hoped for. Spotting a large silver birch growing on a grassy bank, I went to investigate. It clearly had possibilities, and with some judicious pruning, a well-shaped, tapering trunk could be created. Several major branches that were clearly not required were pruned off and I easily dug the tree up. After the roots had been carefully wrapped in damp newspaper, I placed it in a plastic bag for further protection.

I was delighted that I had collected such a good specimen — far better than I had hoped for — and I started walking back to my car, taking a different route just in case I noticed anything else interesting on the way. What a good plan that turned out to be, because I did spot another tree with potential, this time a downy birch. It was a very strange tree that had been naturally dwarfed by nibbling wildlife, and consequently had a thick trunk, full of character. When digging up this tree, I had to cut some very long roots that had spread several yards (meters) and few fibrous roots existed. I set off for home, pleased with my morning's work.

silver birch
Betula pendula

This birch had the better root system and so I planted it in a very large, deep rectangular bonsai pot to recover and establish. It was placed in a sunny area of the garden to encourage budding, and that spring many new shoots duly appeared. These were allowed to extend while the tree gained strength. By midsummer the tree was growing very strongly and so I thought it prudent to remove growth that was definitely not required, so that more energy could be channeled into the remaining branches. All shoots were wired into shape, since it was easiest to do this while they were still young and flexible. They set in place within weeks, and I then removed the wire because it was beginning to bite. The tree was regularly fed and continued to grow well. That year I wired all the new shoots, and although it was still early days for the silver birch, it was starting to look quite natural. The tree remained in this pot for a further year, where it was lightly pruned in the summer.

In spring I removed the silver birch from its pot and was pleased to find that the roots were in good order. The tree was root pruned, allowing it to be planted in a slightly over-large, rectangular pot that I had recently purchased simply because I liked it so much. Being a light beige color, it matched areas of

Spring Year 1: **I pruned off all the tree's thick branches and a powerful trunk remained, with a good, solid buttress.**

the trunk and was useful to establish a shallower root system. Before it leafed out, the tree was further wired, pruned and shaped. When pruned in the spring, birch do have a tendency to bleed. This is reduced if they are root pruned at the same time, but although alarming, the bleeding is not detrimental to the tree. Sap for birch wine can be actually siphoned directly from a full-grown tree's trunk in spring, causing no harm.

After two years in this pot, the silver birch was planted into a smaller, rectangular pot and it looked far better for not being over-potted. The color of the bark was becoming

Summer Year 1: **Several months later the tree was growing strongly and covered in new shoots as a result of a healthy root system.**

much more silver and now that the main branches were in position I started to develop the side branches. These were wired outward to give the tree much-needed width and a very natural-looking bonsai emerged.

training tip
Birch are prone to die-back and often shed branches in winter. When styling, create a tree that will not be spoiled if individual branches die.

Late Summer Year 1: **To make the bonsai resemble a mature parkland tree, I angled the branches upward to initiate this structure.**

Summer Year 3: **Good branch ramification was forming and I reduced the pot size to encourage a shallower root system. I removed wire from the smaller branches before it began to bite.**

Summer Year 5: **This smaller pot picks up the pink tones in the bark of this young birch and balances well with the overall size and shape. In autumn the leaves turn a buttery yellow, falling to reveal a good, tree-like winter image.**

Style: Informal upright
Height: 36in (92cm)

downy birch
Betula pubescens

I did not have a pot large enough to accommodate this tree's poor root system, which contained several very long roots necessary for its survival. It was therefore planted in a protected area of the garden, where it budded weakly from the ends of the existing branches and struggled to grow that season. Since the tree was still establishing a root system, I did not feed it, but watered it when the ground became dry in the summer.

The next year the downy birch remained in the ground and it grew like a completely different tree, producing strong, new shoots and generally looking much happier. I was relieved that this weak tree had survived the winter and was now growing vigorously. It was left to grow freely for the rest of the year and dug up in late winter so that I could examine the root system. I was able to remove the heavy roots, since it now had much finer roots nearer the trunk, and I planted the tree in a large, rectangular bonsai pot. All the branches were removed to encourage buds to form on the trunk, allowing me to develop a new branch structure.

Buds did appear and were generally well placed, except for a large gap at the top left of the tree, which refused to bud. I kept the new shoots pruned hard, hoping to encourage further budding, but at the end of that year the birch had a large area with no growth. This presented me with a problem. Reassessing the tree's future, I decided that by rotating it 180 degrees the available branches were better placed, and so the back became the front. The gap was still present, although less obvious and now at the top right. I started to grow a shoot in front of the gap, and also one behind to hide this space and make it appear to be well branched all over.

In the spring the tree was repotted into a much smaller, rectangular pot and grew exceptionally well that year. I partially leaf-pruned in early summer, leaving the foliage on the weaker branches to give them extra strength. At this stage the tree was heavily wired and shaped. It remained in this pot for a further year and was then planted in a round pot, which suited the tree. Being smaller, it made the downy birch look much more established and imposing, and the coloring of the bark was picked up by the pot.

training tip
Disguise large areas of trunk without branches by strategically placing foliage from other branches in the required areas.

Late Winter Year 2: **After two years recovering in the ground, the tree was strong enough to be lifted and examined. As expected, many fibrous roots had grown.**

Late Winter Year 2: **The overall root system was very shallow. After removing heavy roots I planted the tree in a large, rectangular training pot.**

Early Summer Year 3: **The bare area at the top left is obvious here. My efforts to encourage budding by pruning hard were to no avail.**

Late Summer Year 4: **With a different front, careful branch positioning and considerable growth, the gap (now top right) was completely disguised.**

Winter Year 6: **I particularly enjoy viewing bonsai covered in snow. For a short space of time they look completely different and magical, with their branches outlined by the snowfall. The downy birch, now in a round pot, is beginning to take on the appearance of a freely growing parkland tree with low, spreading branches.**

Style: Formal upright
Height: 17in (44cm)

ancient boxwood

Buxus sempervirens

This old boxwood tree was originally part of a clump of several tall trees, growing in a corner of a relative's garden. When they first moved into the house, some 40 years previously, the trees were large and very mature. Ten years ago they decided to completely re-landscape the garden and remove these boxwood trees, which were beginning to look rather unkempt. I asked if I could have them since they had great potential for bonsai training. They seemed rather surprised, given that the trees were nearing 14¾ft (4.5m) in height, but happily agreed and I helped them remove the clump that autumn. As I had hoped, the trunks were all separate and not joined together. I roughly shortened the heights with a saw and loaded the trees into my car.

When I arrived home, I studied each trunk in turn and used a sharp saw to reduce the heights further, pruning off all branches. I had often wondered how old these trees were and decided to count the rings on the section of trunk removed from the largest one. As I expected, the rings were very close together since boxwood is a slow-growing species. Using a magnifying glass I carefully counted over and over again, each time reaching more than 110 rings. I was absolutely staggered — I had not imagined that this tree was nearly as ancient. But would it now bud and grow?

This boxwood tree was planted in the ground where I hoped that it would bud well. That spring, lush green buds emerged from many areas of the trunk and the boxwood quickly became a thick, green pole of leaves. It grew in the garden for two years and was then planted in a very large flower pot. I removed most of the surplus shoots and wired the remaining growth to form the future branches. A dense crown was planned to hide the rather obvious chop and the boxwood grew like a

Autumn Year 1: **Newly dug up, the boxwood trees were reduced in height. The upright tree had the greatest potential, with the thickest trunk and most attractive base.**

young sapling, full of vigor. Being slightly tender when grown in a pot, it was well protected that winter in a cold greenhouse and remained in the flower pot for a further year.

After repotting my trees that spring, I was left with a large, rectangular pot that

Spring Year 4: **After two years in the garden to gain strength, the boxwood was planted in a large flower pot and studied.**

Summer Year 4: **Several areas were devoid of buds. To disguise this, some branches were wired upward and outward.**

Spring Year 6: **Now in a bonsai pot, further wiring and refinement began to establish a definite structure for the future.**

seemed ideal for the boxwood. The well-developed root system was pruned and I planted the tree in the pot. I fed it heavily to maintain vigor and the branches continued to grow well, except for the lower right-hand branch that turned rather yellow and sickly looking. I pruned the other branches back hard to divert energy into this branch, and after just over a year it started to bud and began to grow happily once more. The tree was thoroughly wired at this stage, and although it was healthy, growth was slow — after all, it had taken over 110 years to reach just 14¾ft (4.5m)! I decided that now training had been initiated, the tree would benefit from a spell in the garden where I would allow it to grow freely. I prepared a hole, adding well-rotted horse manure.

The boxwood stayed in the garden for two years and this period was definitely beneficial to the tree, which by now was slightly overgrown. I returned the boxwood to its bonsai pot and was pleased to see a very compact and healthy fibrous root system. All downward growth was pruned off to define the foliage masses and the branches were wired.

I have now had the pleasure of owning this tree for ten years. I estimate that it would probably have taken at least five years to reach the height where I sawed through the trunk revealing the growth rings. So, by my calculations, this boxwood is a very old tree of over 125 years, and still with a long life ahead of it as a much-loved bonsai tree.

training tip
If branches do not emerge in the desired positions, wire nearby branches up or down and then outward as required.

Summer Year 10: **After two more years in the garden to speed growth, additional foliage was wired. Top left branches are carefully positioned to disguise the slightly parallel trunk and suggest greater taper.**

Style: Formal upright
Height: 31in (79cm)

a pair of dwarf cedars of lebanon

Cedrus libani nana

I first noticed these trees while walking around a nearby garden center. They were among a group of about 20, all in a sorry state, with many dead branches and much die-back, probably the result of a combination of being potbound, dried out and frost damaged. The cedars were being offered at a reduced price due to their ill health and I persuaded the manager to sell me two for the price of one. I was delighted with my bargain and studied the trees immediately on returning home, confident that I could bring them back to good health.

Summer Year 2: **With careful watering and light feeding, strength was slowly restored to this previously weak cedar.**

triple-trunk cedar

Although not a conventional multi-trunk, since the trunks emerged from above the base, I decided to try to emulate a cedar shape. The tree was planted in a larger flower pot and left untouched for the next year while it gained strength. By summer, health had been restored, so I pruned many unnecessary branches and wired the larger ones.

The following spring arrived and the tree was root pruned and planted in a bonsai pot. The roots were not in a very good condition but adequate, and I was confident that fresh soil would aid their development. I exposed some of the surface roots to improve the buttress. These needed attention, but I decided not to prune them until the tree was established and growing strongly again.

For the first year the tree made little growth. I lightly fed it and the foliage remained green, appearing healthy. The following year showed great improvement. In the spring the branches were covered in new growth and I began to feed it more heavily. I did not prune at all, to allow maximum root development.

Spring Year 3: **After removing all dead roots, I planted the tree in a training pot. Shortly after, I selected another, more pleasing front.**

Autumn Year 5: **Downward needles were pulled to define the foliage masses. The tree was then completely wired, each branch and twig carefully positioned.**

Summer Year 7: **Twice a year this tree rewards me with fresh growth, in spring and in summer. The attractive shoots stand out, as if they were flowers.**

After becoming well established, in the spring of Year 5 I carefully lifted the tree out of the pot and looked at the roots. I was pleased to see that an excellent, healthy root system had now developed. Although not pot-bound, the cedar was obviously much stronger. I repotted into a slightly shallower pot, changing the viewing angle. I improved the base by pruning off some rather ugly surface roots. That summer the tree was growing with vigor and looked very healthy. It was time for some serious refinement. I lightly pruned the shoots, removed some surplus branches and completely wired everything, carefully positioning each twig.

The tree was not repotted until spring two years later (Year 7). I had recently purchased a large, gray, Japanese pot with another bonsai in mind, but while root pruning the cedar, I placed it in this pot purely out of curiosity. I was surprised that the pot suited the tree so well. But what about the tree for which it was originally intended? I decided that the cedar was the better tree and deserved this pot.

Following potting, the cedar was allowed to grow freely to help thicken the trunks. Despite being a dwarf variety, it has made considerable growth over the years, which has improved the overall appearance. It now resembles a natural cedar shape.

training tip
Always ensure that good health and vigor are present before styling.

Early Summer Year 13: **After considerable thinning and refinement, the cedar has taken on a rounder form with the branches well balanced, making it appear more natural and stately.**

Style: Triple trunk
Height: 25in (64cm)

literati-style cedar

I have developed the second of the pair of cedars into a very different bonsai. It was a much bigger tree than the other, with an excellent base and a single, thick trunk. Being a dwarf variety and therefore slow growing, this tree must have taken many years to attain this trunk girth and overall size.

The best viewing angle was easily apparent, showing a good trunk line and branch arrangement. After settling in for a year to regain strength, the next summer I first removed all the dead branches and reduced the height by almost a third, using a suitable side branch to form a new leader. The two main branches were very flexible and with strong wire I was able to bend and twist them downward considerably. A problem with the structure became obvious — there was no suitable back branch low down. The only solution that I could see was to use a shoot from the main right-hand branch to extend behind the tree, dividing this branch into two and giving the impression of another separate branch. I was happy with the overall

shape and thought that one day this was going to make a good bonsai.

When I removed the cedar from its pot in the spring, I found more dead roots than live ones. I pruned off all the dead roots and left everything that looked healthy. The tree responded well and by late spring looked delightful, being covered in its fresh new foliage. That year, my relative inexperience at the time became clear, when I realized that I had potted the cedar toward the wrong side of the pot and the overall image was unbalanced. As the weight of the trunk was predominantly to the left, it should have been potted slightly to the right. This was corrected the following year and the cedar was planted in its first bonsai pot.

Three years later after annual repotting, I realized that the tree was too wide and I drastically reduced the width of most branches to make it appear taller with more depth. This was a definite improvement and a smaller pot was chosen. I lived with this new shape until the summer, when I studied the tree further. The bottom branches with the lack of a "real" back branch were certainly the problem, and I remembered the words of a fellow bonsai enthusiast: "If you have a problem, cut it off,

Summer Year 2: **Growing vigorously, the top had become dominant and needed heavy pruning.**

then you don't have that problem any more!" After serious thought, and confident that the cedar would make a good literati-style tree, I took a deep breath and removed the lowest three branches, leaving behind small, stubby

Spring Year 3: **A large tray was used as a training pot. Cedars can drop needles after a shock; I was relieved when the buds opened.**

Early Summer Year 4: **The newly extended back branch had grown well, but it was not convincing. The tree still looked flat.**

Spring Year 8: **I reduced the width and considered removing the lower branches. I hid them in white paper to assess the tree.**

Spring Year 8: **With much foliage removed, I could confidently root-prune hard. The tree was planted in a more suitable, round, drum pot, typically associated with the literati style.**

jins. Several branches were also cut off nearer the top to lighten the foliage masses and provide important areas of space. The tree was now completely three-dimensional and at last I was happy with this new pine-like image. Several branches were wired and a smaller, round pot was selected for the spring.

The next year, in its new pot, the cedar began to look glorious. After extensive root pruning it continued to grow well. I completely structured and wired all of the branches, thinning them out as I went and removing downward-pointing needles. Feeding was reduced to minimize growth and I felt that this tree had finally evolved.

training tip

Before removing a major branch, mask it off using white paper and set the tree on a turntable to view from all angles. This will make the result easier to visualize.

Early Summer Year 13: **After much wiring, thinning and refinement, this cedar has taken on the appearance of an aged, tall pine tree. The elegant, well-shaped trunk exhibits excellent taper, and with fewer branches, the cedar looks more three-dimensional.**

Style: Literati
Height: 30in (76cm)

false cypress group planting

Chamaecyparis lawsoniana 'Ellwoodii'

One day many years ago I noticed a neighbor pruning a specimen dwarf cypress that was growing in his front garden. I asked if I could have one of the branches that had been removed, so that I could take some cuttings. It being late winter, I was not sure if they would root, but I did not want to miss out on this opportunity to propagate new stock as I had been planning a group planting and these could be used. From the one branch I was able to take almost 30 separate cuttings of different sizes, and I inserted them into a gritty soil mix in a small seed tray. Later that year they were all showing signs of life. I had certainly hoped that a few would root, but had not expected all of them to be successful.

The cuttings remained in the seed tray for two more years, where they established good root systems. With so many small cypress trees now available, a group planting was certainly possible and a bonsai pot was selected. During their first year they quickly outgrew the pot and I searched for a more natural solution. I obtained an old rectangular slate roof tile at a junk yard and using a large pair of pliers carefully shaped the edges to create the look of a piece of slate collected from a quarry. The next year I removed the group from its pot and the root mass was dense with fine roots. I then proceeded as if it were a single tree, lightly root-pruning. Small holes were drilled in the center of the slate to provide drainage and to enable the group to be secured with wire ties.

For the next five years the group was allowed to extend slowly, with constant pinching. The trees at the sides and back were trimmed harder, to ensure that they would remain smaller than the rest, creating a feeling of depth. Conversely, several of the trees nearer the front were not pruned at all for two years, to make them grow larger than the others in order to further enhance the perspective. Over the next few years the trees began to form a unit. They were regularly thinned out, so that the trunks remained slender and did not become too thick, creating the desired effect of a group of tall trees.

The group was now root-bound and it became difficult for water to penetrate the mass of roots. I regularly submerged the group in a large container full of water, which was effective but tiresome. In the meantime, the group was beginning to outgrow the slate and it was time to find a large pot. I had several spare shallow pots and placed the group in each one to see which was the most suitable. It was clear that a large, oval pot was ideal and in spring the group was root pruned and planted in this pot. The extra depth of the pot gave the trees a more balanced, stable appearance and made watering easier.

Spring Year 3: **Just two years old, the cuttings had strong root systems. The young trees were moved to a shallow, oval bonsai pot, where I arranged them in a group planting.**

Early Spring Year 4: **The slate was prepared by making a retaining wall around the edge with garden clay and peat. I positioned the trees, careful not to obscure any trunk.**

Summer Year 5: **I removed all the unnecessary inner branches and pruned several others to expose more trunk lines. The overall effect was very natural and pleasing.**

This method has proved an easy way of establishing a realistic group planting from very humble beginnings. The trees look good all year round and are always undemanding. It gives me a great deal of satisfaction when I view my group of 29 trees to consider that the only cost incurred has been the price of the pot they are now growing in.

training tip
When creating a group planting, position larger trees at the front and smaller trees behind, to create the feeling of perspective.

Late Spring Year 11: **When transferring to a pot, I added slow-release fertilizer pellets to the soil to keep the trees green and healthy. They will receive no further feeding during the growing season to keep growth to a minimum; I will not allow the trunks to get much thicker. With this in mind, I thinned out the foliage considerably.**

Style: Group
Height: 19in (49cm)

hinoki cypress trio

Chamaecyparis obtusa 'Kosteri'

One summer Sunday afternoon I was driving to a large aquatic center to gain inspiration for my planned koi pond, and stopped off at a garden center. While walking around the outside display area, I noticed a large garden specimen hinoki cypress in the rockery section. I was not too excited at first, since I have seen many similar hinokis (variety 'Nana Gracilis') with large, unsightly basal swellings as the result of grafts, which are therefore not suitable for bonsai. I looked at the label and was intrigued since I was not familiar with this particular variety — 'Kosteri'. On examining the trunk, I was surprised to find no such swellings and began to dig around the base with my fingers, expecting to find an ugly graft hidden under the soil. However, the buttress and root flare were nicely proportioned. The trunk was solid and pleasantly shaped, and the branches were evenly distributed. I decided that I had made quite a find and purchased the hinoki. Needless to say, I never reached the aquatic center that day and headed straight for home, where I spent a long time styling the tree the following day.

While working on the tree, I began to think about my good fortune in discovering this hinoki cypress. Having visited the garden center only several months before, I knew that it was new stock and must have been purchased from a wholesale nursery where possibly many more such trees existed. What an exciting thought! I called the garden center and they agreed to order five more trees for me to assess with a view to further possible purchases.

Two weeks later I returned to the garden center to examine the new batch of hinokis. I immediately discarded the first two trees, both made up of several thin trunks with poor bases and appearing much younger than the hinoki I had purchased before. Feeling somewhat despondent, I carried on looking at the others. The next tree had much more to offer. It had two trunks with the second, smaller trunk joining at the well-developed base. The fourth tree was too sparse for bonsai training, but the fifth had good, well-placed branches and a tapering, single trunk, displaying attractive curves. I had found two new hinokis that showed real promise.

When I arrived home, I lined up my two new trees next to the first hinoki. Although when first purchased it was difficult to tell them apart, since they looked merely like bushes of thick, green foliage with no visible trunks, I decided that it would be an interesting project to style them quite differently, so that I would end up with three very individual and unique trees.

powerful upright hinoki

This was the first hinoki that I had purchased. After my usual photographic session, work began. The front was identified by a combination of trunk shape, root flare and main branch positions. These were all most promising at one particular angle, so the front was easily selected. I pushed a wire peg into the soil as a marker. Next, I pruned off everything that I knew was unnecessary — poor or dead branches and twigs as well as any foliage not usefully placed. This is a good method to adopt when styling raw material because the remaining tree can then be viewed much more easily.

My next step was to start work on each branch, working my way up from the bottom. The main branch had much die-back in the center and this was remedied by wiring foliage from other parts of the branch into this bare area. Each individual branch and shoot was wired and carefully positioned. Slowly the tree began to take shape.

Summer Year 1: **When purchased, the tree was a mass of green foliage. Light was unable to penetrate the dense branches, so the innermost growth had started to die back.**

Summer Year 1: **One day later, many of the branches had been removed. Wiring and shaping the remaining foliage changed this shrubby bush into a tree.**

As I became more familiar with the tree, it was obvious that many branches were not needed, and these were pruned off as I went. The top of this hinoki had several heavy branches that were removed to leave a much finer structure and this was shaped to create a strong crown. When wiring and basic styling were complete, the tree was finalized by adjusting any branches that I had knocked while wiring others and making sure that each branch related well as a whole. I was delighted with the result, which was certainly going to become a very powerful, informal upright bonsai. The tree remained in the flower pot for the rest of the season.

When I started repotting trees the next year, a large, rectangular pot became free. I thought this would make a very suitable training pot for the hinoki and I lifted the tree from its flower pot to examine the roots. It was beginning to become potbound and was full of fibrous roots. Since so much foliage had been removed when styling the tree, I was able to cut off a proportionate amount of roots, and so approximately half were pruned. The hinoki was then angled slightly more upright and looked stunning in its first bonsai pot.

training tip
Garden centers can be a source of excellent potential bonsai trees. Regular visits and the confidence to make inquiries are highly recommended and often help to find raw material that, with time and patience, can result in good bonsai — as clearly illustrated by these three hinoki cypress trees.

Summer Year 3: **Two years later the tree is still growing in its training pot, since I have yet to find the ideal bonsai pot to make the tree look its absolute best.**

Style: Informal upright
Height: 30in (76cm)

twin-trunk hinoki

This tree was destined to be a twin-trunk from day one. The proportions of the trunks were excellent and it evidently had the potential to become a tall, elegant bonsai.

All heavy branches were pruned off, leaving much younger branches behind, which would be in keeping with the trunks. This resulted in over three-quarters of the tree's foliage being removed. The second trunk needed to be repositioned so that it was closer to the main trunk, and heavy wire was applied to move it successfully. Following this, the tree was transformed after I had wired and shaped each branch.

In the spring I selected a large, rectangular training pot for the hinoki and carried out the necessary root pruning so it could be potted. It made good growth during the rest of the season and was not pruned, encouraging the roots to grow strongly and recover.

With a good fibrous root system in place, I was able to reduce the depth of pot further. Its present shallow, oval pot is much more suitable for the tree's slender, elegant form.

Early Summer Year 9: **The lower branch stubs were reduced to much smaller jins, so as not to detract from the main feature of the bonsai — its two trunks.**

Style: Twin trunk
Height: 29in (74cm)

Summer Year 1: **In its large flower pot, it was just possible to see the tree's two trunks beneath the dense growth.**

Autumn Year 1: **The hinoki was styled, and a third trunk pruned hard to become a jin.**

Early Summer Year 2: **String secured the tree in its first training pot as the roots became established.**

cedar-style hinoki

It is usual when styling bonsai to get into a routine of structuring trees with horizontal branches by selecting first branch, second branch, etc., with the danger of ending up with a run-of-the-mill tree if care is not taken. I envisioned something exceptional with this tree and wanted to create a cedar-like image with upward-growing branches and flat pads of foliage. With the wiring and shaping completed, this image was achieved and I felt that I had created a very different hinoki cypress.

When it was time to plant the hinoki into a bonsai pot, I chose a deep, rectangular one to accommodate the roots. It grew in this pot for one year, after which it was given a much more shallow and sympathetic rectangular pot. It remained in this pot for the next three years and was repotted once during this time.

training tip
Gradually reduce the depth of training pots over a period of years before selecting the final shallow pot. This stage should not be rushed.

Early Spring Year 9: **When moving the tree into its rectangular pot, I decided to change planting position. Although the top of the tree curved to the left, the base and weight of the tree were to the right. So, I moved the hinoki to the left where it now looks much more balanced.**

Style: Informal upright
Height: 29in (74cm)

Summer Year 1: **When purchased, the tree had more branches than the other hinokis and appeared very bushy.**

Autumn Year 1: **By training the branches up and out, rather than horizontally, a different structure was defined.**

Early Summer Year 2: **Looking graceful in its first training pot, the tree grew well after heavy root pruning.**

cotoneaster cascade
Cotoneaster horizontalis

I found this natural seedling growing at the back of my garden, under an apple tree. It was just over a year old and had a forked trunk that was heavily curved. I dug it up carefully, so as not to damage the small root system, and planted it in a flower pot. I was pleased with my most convenient find and left the tree to establish itself for the rest of the year, feeding it well.

The next year I lightly root-pruned the tree and a larger flower pot was selected, to provide extra room for the roots to spread. I did not prune the branches, so that the strong growth would help to thicken up the thin trunk, and I fed it heavily. Later in the season, as the cotoneaster was becoming rather overgrown, some styling became necessary and the natural curves seemed to lend themselves to the tree becoming a cascade style. The longest shoot was wired as the main trunk, and the shorter trunk was chosen to become the apex of the tree. I was pleased with the resulting shape and the tree remained in the same flower pot for a further year after root pruning that spring. Some long shoots were trimmed to balance the energy flow throughout the tree.

One year later the cotoneaster was potted in a slightly larger flower pot. Several branches were wired into position, but not pruned. The trunk still needed to become thicker and I let the tree grow freely in an effort to achieve this. I also wired the main trunk further, which was now cascading well below the bottom of the flower pot. At the end of the season I heavily pruned the crown that, typical of bonsai trained in the cascade style, had become the most vigorous part. By removing so much growth from the top, more sap could be channeled into the bottom of the main trunk, which had not grown much that year.

By the following season the growth was well balanced. Branches began to extend all over the trunk and, when long enough, were wired into place. That spring the cotoneaster flowered sparsely, but enough to show what a pleasing feature of the tree this would become. Being so tiny, the flowers were in perfect proportion and small berries followed that autumn, together with good, red autumnal foliage. I took advantage of the cotoneaster being a deciduous variety and studied the trunk that winter without foliage. It was becoming quite thick and I removed some unnecessary shoots to show off the good trunk line more strongly.

After a further three years in a flower pot, I found the perfect bonsai pot. Being tall and thin, the depth visually matched the shape of the tree and the soft gold-brown color blended with the trunk. The branches were pruned hard, shortening them so that the tree became much narrower and more downward in appearance. I extensively thinned the apex and completely wired all the branches. Much attention was given to the lowest part of the trunk, which was positioned into a gentle curve reflecting the shape of the main crown. At last, it had become a cascade cotoneaster bonsai.

training tip

Bonsai trees in tall, deep cascade pots with a limited soil surface need especially thorough and careful watering, to ensure that the water reaches all the way to the bottom of the pot. Otherwise, the trees can easily dry out.

Summer Year 2: **The main trunk was wired downward to initiate training in the cascade style.**

Summer Year 4: **After being allowed to become overgrown, the crown started sapping the strength from the rest of the tree.**

Autumn Year 4: **With the crown thinned out, more energy is directed into the main trunk, where branches had been slow to develop.**

Late Spring Year 6: **After a strong pruning, energy throughout the tree was balanced. Its branches were shaped and wired further.**

Late Spring Year 14: **Spring flowers and new foliage are without a doubt this tree's strongest features, berries and autumn foliage a close second. The apex now resembles a small, charming tree in its own right.**

Style: Cascade
Height: 25in (64cm)

aged hollow-trunk common hawthorn

Crataegus monogyna

This hawthorn was found growing on an abandoned building site, where it had been struggling for many years. The site was exposed and consequently the tree's growth had developed more sideways than upward. Being nearly 6½ft (2m) wide and yet just 3¼ft (1m) high, it was a most unusual shape for a hawthorn. The trunk immediately caught my eye, since it was quite large and covered with wonderfully textured bark — it was obviously an old tree. What a find, and it was a twin trunk as well! Since the tree looked like it would have a large tap root, I decided to collect it a year later and dug a trench around it to help with the development of fibrous roots. The following year I returned in the spring to find it covered in berries. I was delighted because I am convinced that there are some hawthorns that simply do not flower, ever. But not this tree, though, and here was the proof.

Early Spring Year 1: **The tree lifted easily and its roots were reasonable. I pruned large branches drastically, so that it would have a good chance of survival.**

With it planted in a big plastic tub, I began to have second thoughts. After all the planning and effort to collect the tree, the twin-trunk arrangement was not pleasing to the eye. Both of the trunks were exactly the same size and shape, and were parallel. Would this hawthorn ever make a good bonsai? I was not convinced, but I thought that, if the tree lived, I would certainly start training it, and see what happened.

After growing it for two years it was time for some basic structuring. There was a definite main trunk, so I reduced the height of the second trunk, slightly carving it. I was not happy with the result, but lived with it for a couple of months while I rethought my plans. I decided that this tree had no future as a twin trunk and so one of the trunks would have to go — but which one? The second trunk was chosen to remain since it had a more interesting shape and I was also pleased with the carving that I had done. I pondered my decision once more and quickly sawed the main trunk off before I changed my mind.

One year later, the tree was repotted into a bonsai pot. A very open soil mix was used because, despite much growth during the previous year, the roots had not thrived. Two years later the roots were still not strong. The tree appeared healthy and was growing well, but there were very few fibrous roots. I changed the pot and soil mix, using mainly akadama and grit.

By now I had found the perfect pot, one that had been handmade in Japan. It complemented both the color and texture of the trunk, but I would only use it if the roots were in good shape, because being smaller, the pot necessitated much root pruning.

I was delighted to find the tree completely pot-bound next spring, with an abundance of healthy, fibrous roots. The new,

Spring Year 3: **I decided the tree's appearance would be greatly improved by removing the left-hand trunk. The scar could be hidden with carving. I removed the tallest trunk and also pruned off all heavy branches, since more suitable shoots were now growing.**

much smaller pot gave emphasis to the strong trunk line and good surface roots. It also made the tree appear much larger and I was happy with the overall presentation. The branches were heavily wired and positioned and now just needed extra thickness to balance the weight of the trunk. The hawthorn was definitely healthy and the autumn color was most rewarding, but would it ever flower?

The following spring the hawthorn was exhibited for the first time at a national exhibition. I decided not to repot, hoping to encourage flowers by keeping the tree potbound. Bone meal was also applied in the autumn and high-potash fertilizers in the spring, but the only buds that appeared were leaf buds. The foliage masses were thinned out so that balance with the hollowed trunk was maintained.

In the spring two years later I decided that, although there had been no sign of flowers, the hawthorn needed to be repotted since it was obviously very potbound. By now I had given up on the idea of flowers. Maybe it was simply not going to happen — and then it did! Just one flower appeared, but the next year there were many more.

Summer Year 4: **I removed the remaining tap root and selected the required branches, wiring them. This tree was at last showing some potential. When the wire was removed only weeks later, the young branches stayed in position.**

Late Spring Year 6: **The carving was improved and treated with lime sulfur, to bleach and preserve the dead wood. I toned down the bright white with strong coffee. Now in a shallower pot, the overall appearance was more convincing. It was hard to remember that this tree had two trunks.**

Late Spring Year 13: **The branches are kept fairly short and the foliage is regularly thinned, since the bonsai portrays an old damaged and weathered tree that would be unlikely to support strong, lush growth. Despite this image, the hawthorn looks very delicate in spring when the flowers arrive.**

Style: Hollow trunk
Height: 18in (46cm)

multi-trunk common hawthorn

Crataegus monogyna

This strange hawthorn first came to my attention many years ago, when I noticed it growing on the top of a stone wall while on a country walk. It was fascinating how the trunks had formed such twists and curves, actually joining together in several places. One branch even appeared to grow straight through a trunk and out the other side. I dismissed this tree since I felt it was just too bizarre and I also had no idea who owned that particular stretch of wall.

Three years later I was enjoying the same walk one winter morning when I noticed a man repairing the stretch of wall, which was beginning to fall down in places. The hawthorn was still there, looking even stranger without its canopy of leaves. I asked what would become of the hawthorn when he reached that part of the wall, which was in disrepair. He said that it would be discarded and I immediately offered my services in

Early Spring Year 1: **Branch structure often takes on a similar appearance to the tree's roots, certainly the case with this hawthorn.**

helping him dispose of the tree. I removed all the stones around it only to find that it was surviving in virtually no soil at all. The roots mirrored the growth above and were similarly twisted and contorted.

I planted the hawthorn in a large plastic half-barrel, deep enough for the long root system, which had few fibrous roots. I pruned some of the top growth so that when it leafed out there would be less foliage to support and anxiously waited for spring to arrive. The tree responded well to being transplanted and was soon completely covered in rich green leaves. That year all growth was left unpruned so that the tree would gain strength and the root system would consequently improve. I regularly applied a weak solution of balanced fertilizer.

In late spring the next year I felt that the tree had sufficiently recovered for initial styling to commence. I carried out some major pruning and two months later the tree was covered in healthy new shoots. These were thinned out and wired horizontally as new branches, slightly curved to reflect and emphasize the trunk shapes. Any new shoots were removed as and when they appeared. The branches began to thicken and were not pruned for almost two years, while the tree remained happily growing in the barrel.

Spring arrived and I decided that it was time to inspect the roots. As expected, the barrel was full of fibrous roots and I was safely able to remove all the long tap roots, allowing the hawthorn to be planted into a bonsai pot. I had several pots available, but one seemed a particularly good match, blending with the gray-brown trunk coloration. In its new, shallow bonsai pot, the tree showed real potential and I began to wonder if it would ever flower.

Summer Year 1: **The hawthorn had probably never been so healthy and happy, with all this fresh, new soil — much better than a stone wall.**

Summer Year 2: **I removed all the straight, upward branches so that the trunk curves, clearly the tree's main feature, became dominant. New shoots soon followed.**

Late Summer Year 2: **I wired new growth to form spreading branches, and created two crowns at different heights.**

It has remained in this pot ever since, being repotted only once during that time. The growth is pruned each summer and the branches are thickening and gaining some much-needed weight. In Year 10 I was thrilled to find three flower buds, one on each trunk, and several berries followed that autumn. In Year 11 there were more flowers, well distributed among the branches. I hope that a trend has now been set, with more flowers to come every successive year.

Late Spring Year 11: **The hawthorn's trunk lines are truly unique, having been shaped by nature. A well-developed crown and spreading branches soften the strong trunk curves.**

Style: Twisted multi-trunk
Height: 24in (61cm)

european beech

Fagus sylvatica

I was walking around a friend's garden one day and mentioned that I was on the lookout for a large beech tree, knowing full well that such a tree was growing among other larger trees in a corner of his extensive garden. The tree was being outgrown by the other trees and because of the lack of light had few branches. He immediately thought of this tree and kindly said that if I was prepared to help him dig it up, I could take it home with me that afternoon. I investigated the beech and, although it had a general lack of taper, it did have the signs of a good buttress. The trunk was slightly fluted and as it was autumn, it could be lifted safely.

The only problem was the tree's size. At around 14¾ft (4.5m) in height and growing in close proximity to other larger trees, I thought that its removal was likely to be a challenge. I was right. After half an hour of carefully digging deeply around the trunk, the tree still remained firmly in the stony ground. Stronger measures were needed and my friend decided that maybe leverage would be the answer and started to climb up the tree. As he swayed backward and forward near the top, his extra weight helped to loosen the roots and the tree soon uprooted, with my friend jumping to safety. I would not, however, recommend this method, since there are obvious dangers, both to the person and the tree.

The trunk was shortened to 21in (53cm) by sawing through at a suitable point, leaving no branches, and the ripped roots were pruned. I returned home and immediately planted the stump in a sunny area of my garden, wondering what the spring would bring.

After most of my bonsai trees had begun to leaf out in the spring, the beech stump showed no signs of life. I was convinced that it was dead and scratched the trunk to remove a small amount of bark, revealing that it was still green underneath and very much alive. Several weeks later I was thrilled when I noticed buds beginning to form. There were not many, but they were well spaced up the trunk and I began to see possibilities. Over the next few months the new buds opened and the shoots grew strongly.

As the tree had grown so well the previous year, I decided to begin its training in a pot. When spring arrived, I planted it in a rather "attractive" yellow bucket. After the shoots had grown more later that year, they were partly wired for the first time. There were only five main branches and these were positioned reaching upward and allowed to grow unchecked, so that each branch would fill the large spaces in between.

The beech remained in the bucket for two years until it began to resemble a tree. I decided that it warranted a bonsai pot and in the spring examined the roots to see if it would tolerate a much shallower pot. The roots had grown well and the bucket was full of fibrous roots, which had even grown through the styrofoam layer that I had filled the lower half of the bucket with. I pruned the largest downward roots and was left with a good, evenly distributed root system that allowed the tree to be planted in a large, rectangular bonsai pot. The pot matched the tree well, with plenty of room for the roots to grow, and the overall appearance was very satisfying. I did not realize quite how suitable the pot color was until the following autumn, when the color perfectly matched the dry autumn leaves that the beech retained throughout winter.

One year later (Year 5), and with the beech now growing strongly, it was time to wire the branches further. A well-rounded crown helped the tree appear mature and it began to look very natural.

Three years later and the ramification of the fine branches has been allowed to develop slowly. The tree is fed only lightly and the new spring shoots are pinched as the apical buds unfurl, helping to create a more twiggy structure. My friend has watched this tree's development with interest and has assured me that he will not attempt to climb it again.

Early Spring Year 2: **After a year in open ground, I planted the beech in a large bucket in preparation for training.**

Early Summer Year 5: **Not pruning growth helped form a strong root system. Unnecessary side shoots were removed and remaining branches wired. The tree looked as if it had more than just five branches.**

Winter Year 8: **The beech offers year-round interest, with fresh, apple-green shoots in spring, lush green leaves in summer, yellow autumn color and crispy, orange-brown leaves all winter.**

Style: Informal upright
Height: 38in (97cm)

naturally stunted european ash

Fraxinus excelsior

Driving to visit a friend one spring afternoon many years ago, a small tree growing on an old wall caught my eye. It was living outside a house and right next to the road. I had very few bonsai at that time and was eager to increase my collection, but being in a hurry, I planned to have a closer look on my journey back. When I returned, the owner was in her front garden pruning roses. The tree was a naturally stunted ash, which must have struggled to survive for many years. It was very dirty and grimy from passing traffic, but had an interesting shape and potential. I politely explained my interest to the owner and asked if I could rescue the tree from certain eventual death. She said that she had no interest in the tree and was amused when I said that it would be going to a good home. I carefully pulled the ash from its pocket of soil and crumbling mortar, thanked the owner and set off for home.

The trunk of the ash was thoroughly washed and scrubbed, revealing a very interesting texture to the bark. I expected it to be smooth, but a large area was pitted, giving the tree an aged look. The compact root system enabled it to be planted in a large bonsai pot. I angled the trunk heavily so that it could be trained in the slanting style. At that time it was the largest tree in my collection — about 19¾in (50cm) tall — and without doubt the most impressive as far as I was concerned, although I was quite aware that ash is not one of the most suitable species for bonsai cultivation, with its fairly large, pinnate leaves and coarse growth.

Three years passed and the tree had grown well during that time. I leaf-pruned it annually and the leaves were reducing in size. Every year in early spring the apical buds were removed, prompting the smaller buds to grow and resulting in more compact leaves.

As my knowledge increased, I realized that the surface roots were a very poor example for a bonsai tree. They resembled a pair of legs rather than the convincing roots of an old tree. I turned the tree around and decided that a more suitable front would actually be the current back of the tree. At this angle the roots appeared less ugly. The trunk was positioned slightly more upright and the pot was changed for a shallower slate-blue oval. These were definite improvements.

Five years later, I realized that I was never going to be happy with the root structure of the tree. The roots were an eyesore and had to be improved if this tree was ever going to become a reasonable bonsai. Late that spring I removed a large ring of bark directly above the roots and painted this with hormone rooting liquid. The whole tree was then planted in a large flower pot and buried up to the first branch. It was now potted vertically, which seemed to suit the tree more — I had only previously planted it in the slanting style because it made the large, ugly roots appear to be supporting the angle. That year the ash grew slowly and the soil was never allowed to become dry. Everything appeared to be going well with the tree and I was eager to see if new roots were forming, but decided to wait until early spring to see what was happening under the soil.

Spring arrived and it was time to examine the ash's roots. I removed the tree from its flower pot and was pleased to discover that it

> ### training tip
> Remove strong apical buds on ash trees in late winter to activate weaker, dormant buds, consequently reducing leaf size and promoting back budding.

Summer Year 1: **Six months after collection the ash tree was established as a slanting-style bonsai. It was not pruned for the first year to gain much-needed strength.**

Summer Year 5: **With a new pot, different front and less-severe potting angle, the overall appearance improved, but the surface roots were still poor.**

was completely potbound. The soil was carefully brushed away to reveal an excellent arrangement of surface roots. They were well established and evenly spaced around the trunk base, looking natural. The exercise had been a resounding success, transforming the tree's worst feature into its best. The ash was then planted completely upright in a small, oval bonsai pot. A large branch on the right was also pruned back to a younger shoot that was more in scale with the rest of the tree. It had started to take on a completely new appearance.

Summer Year 11: **After layering, the resulting surface roots were now exceptional and looked very convincing. They helped the ash appear more natural and solid.**

Summer Year 13: **This bonsai has an interesting shape in winter, but it is without doubt best viewed in leaf. The pinnate leaves resemble small branches and twigs covered in dainty leaves. By removing new apical buds and leaf pruning in early summer, the leaves have been reduced considerably and are in scale with the overall tree.**

Style: Informal upright
Height: 19¼in (49cm)

candle-flame maidenhair tree

Ginkgo biloba

The ginkgo is a much misunderstood tree, thought by many to be more of a curiosity than suitable as bonsai material. Despite having leaves and being deciduous, it is in fact closely related to the conifer family. The tree has a fascinating history, being the sole survivor of a group of trees that flourished over 350 million years ago, hence one of its alternative names "fossil tree." The ginkgo seems to be a species that is either loved or hated by bonsai growers. Personally, I have never understood how anybody could not be drawn to this undemanding and rewarding tree.

A bonsai enthusiast from our local society announced that he was selling some of his trees. I had heard that he owned a ginkgo and the next day I visited him. His ginkgo did indeed have the potential to be a good specimen and was, to my mind, his best bonsai. I could not believe my luck. The tree had an interesting, aged trunk, containing many "chichi" (trunk nodules), showing that it was very old and estimated to be around 80 years at that time. Although it was late summer, the branches were sparse and he said that it had not grown well that year since it was probably potbound. I decided that I would never be able to create a mature trunk like this from a sapling ginkgo and was pleased that the bonsai needed much work, so that I had the opportunity to improve it myself.

Once back home I began exploring the ginkgo's possibilities. I really disliked its bright blue "fruit bowl"-shaped pot and ordered a large, round, drum pot. When it arrived that spring, the ginkgo was carefully removed from its existing pot and I could not have imagined what I was going to find. I was completely stunned when almost all the soil fell off, together with many decayed roots, leaving only a few large roots and virtually no fibrous roots. Despite having been under cover for a while, the peaty soil, which contained hardly any grit, was sodden and the tree was in a very sorry state. I was convinced that this ginkgo was destined for the compost heap, but was desperate to try and save it. All rotten roots were removed, leaving very little supportive root behind. The tree was planted in its new bonsai pot rather like a giant cutting, using a very gritty, free-draining mix. I planted it more upright, tied it in well, since having so few roots it was very unstable, and waited apprehensively to see if any buds would swell.

I was aware that ginkgos are often late to leaf out and did not give up hope when my other bonsai started to grow and the ginkgo showed no signs of life. During its convalescence it was misted regularly and positioned in a cold, light greenhouse, protected from hard frosts. Just as I was beginning to worry, I noticed that the lower buds had begun to show signs of green at their tips, although the top of the tree still

Late Summer Year 1: **There was certainly a more pleasing front than the existing one, and if the trunk was angled upright, a better line could be shown. The blue pot would definitely have to be changed.**

appeared dormant — or possibly dead. My patience, however, was rewarded and the tree leafed out all over in a matter of weeks. Ginkgos would not have survived on this planet for so long had they not possessed such a strong will to live. I moved it outside and watered sparingly. The buds on the main part of the trunk were not growing at all, only the lower shoots. This was very unusual since a tree's most vigorous part is normally at the top, but not with this ginkgo, which had only one weak shoot growing in this area. I let the lower shoots grow unchecked all season so that the almost non-existent root system could begin to recover.

A year later the main trunk was still refusing to grow. It was clear that the tree was healthy at this stage and so I completely leaf-pruned

Spring Year 2: **A few months after the lower shoots began to extend, I fed the ginkgo lightly with a weak liquid fertilizer. The tree was making a miraculous recovery and responded well.**

Autumn Year 5: **Over several weeks, the heart-shaped leaves slowly changed to vibrant yellow. When the last leaf turned, the tree looked glorious for just a few days, before all the leaves suddenly dropped.**

all of the bottom shoots to force much-needed strength back into the top of the trunk, but it still would not grow. I was convinced that persistence with this technique would pay off and leaf-pruned the lower shoots for the next two years, allowing very little growth in this area. It was frustrating, since I badly wanted the lower shoots to extend and become tall subsidiary trunks, to create an unusual clump style and improve the shape of the bonsai. The following spring arrived and the roots remained untouched. To my delight, although still leafing out later than the rest of the ginkgo, shoots began to grow from all over the top. Strength had been restored and the tree had responded exactly as I had hoped, although it had taken longer than expected. Feeding heavily, I allowed the lower shoots to extend, forming tall trees around

the main trunk. The overall structure was greatly improved and I wired many of the shoots into place, creating the classic ginkgo "candle-flame" style. At this stage the bonsai was exhibited at a national show and received many favorable comments.

After growing well in the bonsai pot for a total of five years, I decided to root-prune that spring and was encouraged to see that the tree was completely potbound, being full of healthy, thick coniferous-like fibrous roots. A hard root prune was carried out and the tree grew well that year, with even growth all over. By now the height, including the pot, was over 3¼ft (1m) and the bonsai was becoming difficult to transport to exhibitions and society meetings. It has therefore not been shown publicly for several years.

Despite a poor start, the ginkgo has performed exceptionally well. Over the years I have come to know this tree intimately and am now able to control and predict its growth. The fact that it receives no insect or disease attacks is an added bonus. If I had to choose just one of my bonsai to keep, my ginkgo would without a doubt be that tree.

training tip
Use an extra-gritty, free-draining soil mix to improve poor root systems.

Early Spring Year 9: **The ginkgo was wired to open out the trunks and branches, making the tree appear slightly wider and not as tall.**

Summer Year 9: **In full leaf, the classic ginkgo "candle-flame" style can clearly be appreciated. Over the years, the leaf size gradually reduced as a result of pruning, pinching and leaf trimming, and is now in perfect scale with this very large tree. If I had to choose just one of my bonsai to keep, my ginkgo would without doubt be that tree.**

Style: Candle-flame
Height: 38in (97cm)

driftwood-style needle juniper

Juniperus rigida

I first noticed this needle juniper while visiting a bonsai nursery one spring. Recently imported from Japan, it was obviously suffering, with the foliage being very yellow and weak. It was tucked at the back corner of a large group of lush green needle junipers and, to my good fortune, was going unnoticed. I could see that the tree had great potential; indeed, if it lived it would probably become the finest needle juniper there. The driftwood had a dramatic, flowing shape, the trunk was solid and the base was good. The branch structure was poor, however, and there was an odd second trunk that was begging to be removed. The foliage mainly consisted of three small pads of pale growth,

much of it dead with no signs of any new buds. I began to see the chance of a bargain and convinced myself that even if the tree did not survive, I would be left with an excellent piece of driftwood. Capitalizing on the tree's general ill health and sad appearance, a deal was struck. I would not normally recommend such action, but the tree had fired my imagination and I had always wanted a quality needle juniper.

I thought that the tree had been traumatized by its recent long journey and decided to leave repotting until the next year when it would hopefully be stronger. It was kept under cover, out of the rain. Since the sodden soil indicated poor drainage, I watered it very carefully. After about four weeks, to my delight, some new green buds started to appear on the top of both live areas. The important lower branch, however, continued to deteriorate with no signs of life. I began to worry that the top of the strange second trunk might be sapping energy from this branch, so off it came, leaving behind a nice jin. The highest branch continued growing, albeit slowly, but the main lower branch began to turn more yellow and soon died.

I inspected the roots and was horrified to see how potbound the tree was. There were roots over 5ft (1.5m) long, coiled around and around the bottom of the pot. I was annoyed at myself for not having checked them in the spring and immediately transplanted the tree into a larger pot, not root pruning because it was early summer.

In the spring the tree was root pruned and planted in a new, larger training pot. It was then fed heavily for the next four years. The surviving branch grew well, giving the tree much-needed strength. At this stage I began to study the tree from all angles and discovered a new front, one that I had never

Summer Year 5: **Now the tree required structuring, but I had no clear ideas. My previous design was fine — until the lower branch died. New growth would benefit from pruning, to increase the tree's strength. I began to contemplate a change of front.**

Early Spring Year 1: **Though in poor health with no structure, the superb shape of the driftwood made this juniper very attractive. It showed great potential.**

Summer Year 5: **It was soon apparent that this was by far the best viewing side of the needle juniper. The lower branch dying was a blessing in disguise. Had it lived, I probably would never have looked to change the front.**

noticed before, since I had previously selected the front when the tree still had its lower branch. There was a problem though — the top of the driftwood was strongly angled backward and to the right, throwing the balance. Maybe this could be corrected by using a heat-bending technique. This method of using steam to bend dead wood is commonly used in furniture making. I wrapped the area of dead wood with wet paper toweling, then tightly bound it with aluminum foil. The live area of the tree was protected with more foil and I proceeded to move the flame of a lighter around the sealed area. Soon, steam started to appear. After ten minutes I carefully began bending the top of the trunk, which had become surprisingly pliable. With wire, I tied the tip in place to the trunk, unwrapped the foil and tissue and carefully dried the area with the flame. The wire was removed and the upper trunk remained in its new position. I had successfully bent the dead wood more than 3in (8cm), transforming the whole tree. There was now so much foliage from the one remaining branch that I was able to treat it as a high secondary trunk. I wired everything and positioned several nicely shaped sub-branches. At last I was making progress with this tree.

During the winter I selected a quality gray pot. Spring arrived and the tree was repotted, with the new front that I had chosen. The overall appearance changed dramatically, with the pot complementing the driftwood needle juniper.

training tip
When unsure of how to proceed with styling, leave the tree in a prominent place to look at from different angles over a period of time so that all options can be given due consideration.

Summer Year 7: **Still in development, the tree will need constant pinching and refinement to further define the foliage masses. A well-balanced structure has been achieved — and more importantly, so has good health and vigor.**

Style: Driftwood
Height: 34in (86cm)

juniper cascade

Juniperus squamata 'Blue Carpet'

This is one of the first trees that I ever trained, and I find it satisfying that after many years it has become a very natural looking cascade-style bonsai. The juniper started life as a small, rooted cutting. After letting it grow for only a year, I was keen to wire it in a shape of some kind, but had no clear style in mind. The result was a small and twisted, informal upright tree. The next day, however, I decided that the juniper would be better suited growing in a cascade manner, and so the trunk was bent downward and initial training commenced. This was an improvement and I was pleased with my decision.

One year later I had lost interest in this tree, having so many other potential bonsai trees that seemed more important. I decided that the juniper belonged in the garden and so I planted it in a corner of my rockery.

Autumn Year 2: **I removed the wire that shaped this tree downward and planted it in the ground. This was the best decision I could have made; there it stayed, vigorously growing an attractive silvery green mat of foliage.**

Four years later I was more experienced in growing and styling bonsai and my interest in larger trees was developing. By now the juniper had made so much growth that there was a danger of it taking over the rockery completely. The branches had extended and the foliage was lush. On studying the tree closely I realized that perhaps there really was potential in this tree after all, and one day in the spring I decided to dig it up. I was amazed at how thick the trunk had become, with a most attractive downward curve. It was potted into a shallow plastic container, pruned heavily so that there would be less foliage for the roots to support and some of the branches were wired into shape.

While on holiday, I looked around a garden center and found a deep, Chinese-style pot. I am not normally keen on decorated pots, but the characters on the sides were fairly discreet. Even better, the pot was very reasonably priced, and so I purchased it with my cascade juniper in mind.

I planted the juniper in the new bonsai pot in the spring and then pruned and wired the foliage masses, expecting it to grow well that season, but it failed to do so. In fact, it hardly grew at all and looked rather unhealthy. I was puzzled as to why this should be the case. The following year it was not repotted and it perked up slightly, but failed to respond well to feeding, generally looking rather sorry for itself. I moved it to different positions in the garden — full sun, partial shade, full shade — but something was definitely wrong with the tree. Its growth was poor and I began to realize that it must be a root problem. That spring I thoroughly examined the roots and found at the center of the root ball a large amount of heavy clay soil from the garden. The roots had been really struggling in this unsuitable soil and I removed as much of it as I could, replacing it with a very open, gritty mix. Several weeks later the tree began to respond. I was pleased to see it budding well and it has grown strongly ever since.

Last year when positioning the tree on a pedestal, I noticed that it was most attractive when viewed from the side. Having always styled the tree so that the trunk grew in front of the pot, I found this different angle pleasing, and after considering the various options, decided that the side view was the one that I favored.

training tip

Growing trees in the ground for a period considerably accelerates their growth.

opposite top left, Summer Year 7: **Cascade trees usually have an apex, but this juniper lacked suitable branches. One possibility was to create a cascade with no apex, but I felt that if I wired and positioned the top left-hand branch above the base of the tree, a good crown could be formed. The branch was heavily curved above the base and disguised by foliage masses, creating the basis for a balanced crown to form.**

opposite bottom left, Early Summer Year 10: **When I began my yearly repotting, the juniper was planted in its new pot and started to look more like a real cascade-style bonsai, although it still needed a good deal of development. Defined foliage pads were beginning to form as a result of much pinching.**

Summer Year 16: **It is often a good idea to stand back from a bonsai tree and reassess the overall appearance, keeping an open mind, in this case prompting a change to the viewing angle. The tree was restructured, with some branch positions redefined and changed so that they could be better viewed from the side. The cascading shape of the tree now looks much more natural.**

Style: Cascade
Height: 31in (79cm)

garden-hedge dwarf honeysuckles

Lonicera nitida

Garden hedges consist of different types of trees and shrubs, many of which make excellent bonsai material. If, when a hedge is removed, you are in the right place at the right time, it is likely to be your lucky day. Seven years ago my lucky day dawned.

A shrub that makes an excellent, dense evergreen hedge, being easy to clip and keep neat, is *Lonicera nitida*. There must be many potential bonsai specimens hidden in garden hedgerows. Driving past a house in a nearby village I noticed a lady digging up her lonicera hedge. I stopped and politely inquired if it was her intention to dispose of any of the trees. She replied that they were all destined for the garbage dump later that day. I rushed home to fetch my trailer and save her the trouble of discarding them, collecting about two-thirds of the trees. From this large selection there were two loniceras that showed more potential than the rest.

triple-trunk dwarf honeysuckle

This lonicera had a large base and comprised many separate trunks that were growing closely together. It had a good, compact root system and so I planted it in a spare, deep bonsai pot, ideal for training purposes. That year the tree grew with tremendous strength and I fed it heavily to encourage this growth. Thinking that the tree was only wasting energy growing so many shoots that were going to be pruned off after styling, I thinned it out and established a basic structure. I removed several of the trunks that were beginning to grow together and the tree continued to grow strongly for the rest of the season. I wired many of the shoots at the end of the year.

The following spring I had a spare drum pot that I thought would suit the tree. I examined the root ball to ascertain how much I would be able to prune. As I had expected, the tree was completely potbound and the soil was full of roots. I was able to root-prune hard and still leave ample fibrous roots to support the tree. That year the lonicera continued to grow well and I fed it with high-nitrogen fertilizers to maintain strong growth.

Summer Year 1: **Expecting the lonicera to take longer to establish, I was pleased that it was growing so well and was covered in a multitude of new shoots.**

Late Summer Year 1: **Removing several major trunks and many smaller ones opened up the tree. It was more obviously composed of multiple trunks, not just one.**

Spring Year 2: **After repotting the tree, strong surface roots were apparent. Regular trimming and pinching encouraged the foliage pads to develop.**

Three years later I changed the pot to a slightly smaller, round pot with a subtle blue glaze. I let the lonicera grow unchecked to help the branches thicken so that they would appear more mature. At the end of that season the tree had grown too wide and I wanted it to appear taller. I thinned the branches considerably and pruned hard so that it would bud well the following spring, which it duly did.

training tip

Loniceras have vigorous root systems and quickly become potbound. Annual repotting is usually advisable to ensure optimum health.

Summer Year 8: **As a result of heavy thinning and pruning in the spring, new buds emerged full of strength. By summer, the tree looked its absolute best.**

Style: Triple trunk
Height: 21¼in (54cm)

formal upright dwarf honeysuckle

Having a single, well-tapering trunk, this lonicera showed real promise. The foliage was sparse, although the roots were reasonable, so I planted it in a large flower pot and placed it in full sun to aid bud development.

A few weeks later, weak buds began to emerge in several places and the growth was poor. Most of the buds had developed on the top half of the tree, and if this lonicera was ever going to make a good bonsai, it needed a back branch low down, where no buds had appeared. As the tree grew more, I fed it lightly with a weak liquid fertilizer and the lonicera started to grow more strongly, although it failed to bud further. I let the tree grow for the rest of the year and hoped that it would produce more buds, but to no avail, although it looked very healthy.

When I had finished repotting my bonsai trees the following spring, I was left with a large, round pot with a pleasant green glaze. I felt that with some styling this lonicera could become quite presentable and so, after deciding that it was now fully recovered, it was styled, rootpruned and repotted. It looked rather flat, since the main back branch was halfway up the trunk. I noticed a small shoot at the base of this branch and decided that, if it was allowed to grow straight down and tied in tightly to the trunk, I might be able to use this growth to create the desired lower back branch.

A small groove was carved in the trunk and the shoot was tied tightly with raffia. For that season, all other growth was kept trimmed because I wanted the energy to be channeled into my new potential back branch solution.

That year, shoots developed into a definite branch, and I was happy that this had resolved the problem. Even from the back it looked like this branch emerged from the trunk and the raffia was removed at the end of the season. To ensure a good contact with the trunk, the branch was glued into the groove using superglue (strong epoxy resin). As it continued to swell, it would eventually become part of the trunk.

Over the next few years, the lonicera was allowed to grow strongly and then pruned hard in order to develop thick branches with dense foliage.

training tips

• Unsightly trunk curves can be masked by growing strategically placed foliage.

• Allow buds at the base of branches to develop into additional branches to fill gaps, if no alternative is available.

Early Spring Year 1: **I was attracted to this tree by the well-proportioned straight trunk, which would obviously become a main feature. I reduced its height by half and removed heavy branches to promote budding.**

Early Summer Year 2: **I wired all the shoots and shaped the tree, which appeared two-dimensional without a back branch. I trained several shoots to disguise the trunk's front curve and make the upper trunk seem straighter.**

Summer Year 5: **After three years in the green bonsai pot, I planted the lonicera in a larger, more pleasing drum pot for one year.**

Summer Year 5: **This shows the back branch in close-up, created from a shoot much higher up.**

Summer Year 8: **The next year I selected a very formal, rectangular pot that matched the mood of the tree. I am sure that this *Lonicera nitida* will remain in this pot for many years to come.**

Style: Formal upright
Height: 26in (66cm)

"large" dwarf honeysuckle

Lonicera nitida

This *Lonicera nitida* was found in late winter, growing on some empty land that had recently become a building site. I can only think that many years before somebody had dumped lots of hedge clippings there, and because honeysuckle is easy to root, many had. There was a small grove of at least 50 vines, most of which were over 5¾ft (1.75m) tall. I managed to crawl among them and spotted one that instantly appeared to stand out from the rest. The tree was easy to remove and had a good root system. It was heavily pruned, reducing it to around 14in (36cm) in height, and its many fibrous roots allowed it to be potted straight into a deep bonsai pot. The lonicera was then left to recover in a sheltered area of the garden.

It was not long before the tree began to show signs of life and several buds appeared. Normally I allow all collected trees at least one year to become established, often two or more before I start training them. However, by early summer this lonicera was growing so strongly that I decided to proceed with some basic styling. As I began structuring the many long shoots, I soon noticed that there was a large gap in the top right-hand side of the trunk where no buds had developed, so I considered ways of masking the area. I decided to prune back all branches hard, feed the tree heavily and leave it at an angle where this area would face the most direct sunlight. Four weeks later a shoot appeared in exactly the place where one was needed.

The tree was left to grow unchecked for the rest of the year, to thicken the branches. It was repotted the following spring and the roots were found to be in excellent condition. The soil level was lowered slightly to improve the flare of the buttress and expose the surface roots. During the year I kept the branches lightly trimmed, but allowed the leader to grow freely; it needed to thicken considerably to hide the cut where the trunk had been reduced in height. I peeled off some of the bark to reveal a fresh, smooth trunk underneath. Lonicera has flaky bark and is one of the few trees whose loose bark can be peeled off without causing the tree any harm at all.

Just a year later, the tree was already beginning to look as if it had been in training for much longer. The foliage pads were developing nicely and I completely wired every branch and twig on the tree. I spent much time working on the apex because I regard this as one of the most significant parts of the tree. A well-structured crown finishes off the whole appearance.

Early Spring Year 1: **The dwarf honeysuckle had several large base branches that, when pruned off, revealed a thick, well-shaped and nicely tapered trunk.**

Summer Year 1: **To encourage bud production, the tree was moved into a sunnier position and lightly fed. In months it was covered in many substantial shoots.**

Early Summer Year 3: **By using a much shallower pot when the lonicera was repotted, the tree's appearance was greatly improved. The pot's subtle glaze reflected the color of the trunk.**

In the spring I wanted to repot the lonicera and also change the pot. I heavily root-pruned the tree and laid out a selection of possible pots, trying the tree in each one. Some were slightly better, but none were what I had really been looking for. I began to search my bonsai shed to check for any other spare pots and found a pot that I had bought several years ago from a friend, not for a particular tree but simply because I liked it. Being shallower, it was a good match, and the lonicera remained in this pot for the next three years, being repotted every year due to its vigorous habit.

Three years later, the lonicera had become a fine tree, being always very green and healthy. It had outgrown the current pot and it was certainly time for a change. I decided that it would look good in a recently purchased drum pot. It was not as deep as the pot it was replacing and the studs made it look even shallower. But being round, it appeared smaller, and so the overall effect was nothing short of a transformation.

training tip
In order to encourage good budding, position heavily pruned trees in full sun.

Summer Year 7: **For strong, healthy growth, I prune the branches hard each spring when I repot the tree. Regular feeding and a sunny situation ensure well-balanced, dense, lush growth. The lonicera has many small, pale yellow spring flowers that add to its charm.**

Style: Informal upright
Height: 26in (66cm)

"small" dwarf honeysuckle

Lonicera pileata

A fellow bonsai enthusiast who specializes in smaller trees (*shohin*) often exhibited many different specimens of this variety of lonicera. It became obvious to me that she had many such trees and at an exhibition I inquired where she had obtained them. She explained that while visiting a garden center three years previously she had spotted about 15 stocky little loniceras, and since they were all quality material, she had purchased the lot. "Would you like one?" she asked. She had five spare plants put to one side and said I would be welcome to choose one of them if I visited her to collect it. The only drawback was that she lived over 100 miles away, but I decided that it would be a pleasant day out and a chance for me to see her whole collection. This was an offer I could not refuse — I immensely enjoy the chance of seeing other bonsai collections.

It was springtime and the next free weekend I set off early in the morning, feeling very optimistic. When I arrived I could immediately tell that I was at a real bonsai enthusiast's house, spotting the many stock trees growing in her front garden. The back garden contained a wonderful, varied bonsai collection. She led me to the five loniceras, which were lined up for my selection, and I began scrutinizing each one in turn. It was a difficult decision, but after ten minutes I chose one.

The lonicera, although only small, had a very powerful and well-tapered trunk, but the branches were thick and lacking in character. It was not practical to use any of them, so they were all removed.

Several weeks later the tree budded fairly well and I allowed the new shoots to grow freely for the rest of the season. In the winter, after the branches had grown enough for initial structuring, they were thinned out, wired and positioned. I was not happy with the result since, although many branches had grown, most were not in suitable positions for the design that I had in mind. Knowing that I would never be pleased with the branch placement, and after examining all possibilities — including several different fronts — I removed all the branches once more, hoping that the buds would grow in more useful places this time. As soon as the buds appeared I could see that things were looking more promising and I was glad that I had made the decision to start again. The lonicera was covered in many more buds than previously and I needed to thin out the new shoots as they began to grow that summer.

At a local bonsai nursery the following spring I found a formal, rectangular pot that I thought would be ideal for this tree. Small trees have many advantages — they are easy to carry and transport, and also the pots, being smaller, are usually much cheaper. The tree was root pruned hard and moved into this pot, where it has stayed ever since. Over the years I have removed several large branches to give the foliage pads room to develop.

opposite, Early Summer Year 7: **Each spring the tree is radically thinned and old, large, tattered leaves are removed to make way for fresh new shoots and small flowers.**

Style: Informal upright
Height: 10¼ in (26cm)

Spring Year 1: **I selected this tree for its solid trunk and good buttress. The cluttered branches will need to be regrown.**

Spring Year 1: **Loniceras respond well to hard pruning so I decided to remove all the heavy, straight branches.**

Winter Year 2: **The new shoots were well placed, although as ramification developed, several were surplus and removed.**

root-on-rock 'little gem' spruce

Picea abies 'Little Gem'

I used to tour the local garden centers regularly, on the lookout for trees that have the making of a bonsai. On one particular occasion I noticed several balls of tight green foliage growing in small flower pots. Closer inspection revealed that they were five dwarf spruce of the variety 'Little Gem'. At that particular time these plants were quite uncommon. I had no idea what I would do with them, but did not want to regret buying too few, so I bought all five. It was fortunate that there were no more, because in my enthusiasm I would probably have bought a dozen.

I find that I achieve the best styling results when I am feeling creative, and so one rainy day in summer I closely inspected the trees, carefully pulling the branches apart to reveal the trunks. The problem was that the foliage was so dense that it was difficult to see how to proceed, so out came the branch pruners. After styling, I left the trees to grow unchecked for the next year while I considered their future. A couple of the trees were really delightful and I thought that they might make good individual *mame* specimens, or would some kind of group arrangement be best?

The spruce were beginning to grow well and I lightly trimmed them in the winter. They were starting to look so good that it was a shame to hide them away at the back of the garden. The time had come to do something further with them and I decided to plant the trees on a rock that I had recently acquired for this purpose. It was prepared by cutting into the top with an angle grinder and then finished off with a chisel, creating a pocket for soil. A drainage hole, angled toward the back, was then drilled at the bottom of the depression. I root-pruned each tree individually and arranged them in the planting hole on the top of the rock.

Three years later I was asked to exhibit some trees at the Chelsea Flower Show. The spruce trees were at their absolute best and so were immediately my first choice. As it was spring, they were covered in fresh, light green, new shoots that looked almost like flowers. The rock planting, which was displayed in a *tokonoma* setting in a *suiban* that I had recently purchased, looked glorious.

The spruce group is now looking even better. I radically thin it out once a year in the spring and this is all the pruning that it requires. During the summer a second flush of growth can be enjoyed. Every year the group is repotted, and since the roots are now one solid mass, it is treated as if it were one tree. I feed it only lightly so that the trunks do not grow very much — thick trunks would spoil the effect. Despite the small amount of soil, they need no more watering than some of my much larger trees, probably because the rock stands in water.

Spring Year 1: **I knew these trees had potential, but I was unsure of which approach to take. I placed them on a high shelf at the end of the garden where they stayed for two months. I looked at them regularly, thinking of how best to use them.**

Summer Year 1: **I decided to remove all the heavy branches and see what was left. This turned out to be not much at all. I wired the remaining shoots in place.**

training tips

• When creating groups, position branches so that they grow outward, toward the light.

• Stand rock plantings in water to provide humidity.

Early Summer Year 2: **Over 2in (5cm) deep, the planting hole allowed room for the spruce to grow well. With light trimming, they were positioned so that most branches faced outward. The planting began to resemble a group of trees growing atop a large cliff. I displayed the rock in an oval pot filled with gravel until I could find a suitable *suiban*.**

Spring Year 6: ***Picea abies*** '**Little Gem**' is an absolute must for any bonsai grower who likes very small trees or rock plantings. It is undemanding and widely available in garden centers. My spruce group has developed well and lived up to its name, becoming a real "little gem"!

Style: Root on rock
Height including rock: 14½in (37cm)

root-on-rock dwarf spruce

Picea glauca var. *albertiana* 'Conica'

Autumn Year 1: **The young spruce trees were the ideal size — 6–8in (15–20cm) — to begin training.**

This wonderful piece of tufa rock was a prize that I had the good fortune to win in my local bonsai society's evening raffle. Each meeting, the club holds a raffle to raise funds and all the prizes are donated by members. On this particular occasion the prize had been given by a friend of mine and he has been pleased to follow the development of this bonsai.

I was eager to use the rock, which had a very flat base, and decided that a planting of dwarf spruce would be best, particularly since I was aware that my local garden center had recently stocked up with these trees. It was late spring and I had just finished my repotting schedule. Eight small spruce trees were soon purchased and I studied the rock to find the best viewing angle. Being tufa rock — soft and very porous — I was able to carve out planting pockets with a screwdriver. Separate holes were made mainly near or on the top of the rock and each tree was styled and wired. All the lower branches were removed to expose the trunks and make these young saplings take on the appearance of older trees. Each spruce was root pruned and those with branches growing mainly on one side were planted at the edges of the rock, with the branches growing outward, toward the light. The rest were positioned, and with some minor pruning and arrangement of the branches, a rock planting was born.

Late Spring Year 2: **With the trees planted on the rock, the effect was instantly appealing. It was apparent that this group could become very attractive.**

The group recovered in a sheltered area of the garden, where they all quickly budded and began growing, except for one tree that unfortunately died. It was planted at the very front of the rock and, after removing the tree, I decided that it was not necessary for it to be replaced and the resulting hole created an interesting crevice. That summer the remaining seven trees grew strongly and I was finding it difficult to keep them adequately watered. I began looking for a shallow pot and during the winter found an ideal container — an unglazed, oval pot. I inserted screws into the bottom of the rock, wound wire ties around the screw heads and threaded the wire through the pot's drainage holes. This enabled the rock to be anchored firmly in place. The next season I found that the rock dried out much less, since it absorbed the moisture content from the surrounding soil mix, and the trees looked resplendent with their fresh spring foliage. I removed the wire from them, because it was just starting to bite, and I heavily underplanted with moss to create a natural look.

For the next five years, the only maintenance carried out was light shoot-pinching each spring. The trees began to take on a bushy appearance and, now that they were more established, needed restructuring. Over half of the foliage was removed, providing more light for the inner branches and making the spruce resemble trees rather than

Summer Year 7: **With only light pinching each spring, the spruce had become overgrown and needed refinement, although the image was still quite pleasing.**

bushes. Each branch and shoot was wired in a generally horizontal direction and the soil mix in the pot was replaced. I was pleased to see that the roots had grown completely through the soft rock and were now actually growing in the soil as well.

training tip

Tufa rock is ideal for rock plantings, since it is relatively solid, but soft enough to allow planting pockets to be carved by hand.

Summer Year 10: **With less foliage and definite branches, the trees now look more mature. They will not be allowed to become any larger, since they could easily outgrow the rock. The spruce will be kept in check by constant pinching and minimal feeding.**

Style: Root on rock
Height including rock: 17in (43cm)

large formal scotch pine hybrid

Pinus sylvestris

For several years my collection lacked a pine tree. I had never found a suitable specimen, despite much searching. One winter I decided to visit as many garden centers as possible in my quest, but most of the available pines were either very young or displayed bad grafts, which would only get worse as time progressed. I was beginning to give up when I arrived at another plant nursery and immediately noticed a heavily trunked, well-branched pine tree in an oak barrel. It was the centerpiece of their parking lot and was nicely underplanted with cotoneasters and pansies. I felt sure that it would not be for sale and so looked around for similar material, without success. The sales lady asked if I needed any help. I explained that I wanted a large bushy pine tree, rather like the one in the parking lot. Somewhat hesitantly, I asked whether I might possibly be able to purchase it. "Of course!" came the reply. "I'll sell anything when I'm in charge!" We walked over to the tree so that she could tell me how much it would be. I was told that most of the nursery's plants were priced by the size of the pot. She wanted to keep the oak barrel for replanting and went to find a large flower pot. She could not find one big enough, but had a smaller pot and would use that to price the tree! I had found an absolute bargain.

The pine was instantly impressive and on the way home I bought a brown flower pot large enough to plant it in. The tree was very pot-bound and I gently teased out the roots around the edge, planting in a very gritty soil mix, being aware that pines require good drainage.

In the spring the candles began to extend and I pinched out the very tips. By early summer the tree was starting to become overgrown and it was time for styling. The pine was methodically shaped in a typical bonsai image, with horizontal branches forming a triangle. Some newly extended shoots were trimmed with scissors and many large branches were removed. The overall height was not reduced, since the trunk already exhibited good taper.

I purchased a large, rectangular, fairly formal pot that I thought would match the tree's strong image, which was beginning to appear. That spring I removed the pine from the flower pot and combed out the roots with a fork, pruning any that were rather long. I was able to plant the tree in the bonsai pot by removing about one-third of the root ball and expected it to be slow to recover. In a matter of months, however, the pine was covered in fresh new candles and was a wonderful sight to behold. I pinched the candles, removing more as I progressed up toward the more vigorous areas at the top of the tree. That summer several branches began to bud back in bare areas.

In the winter, to extend the foliage pads that were beginning to form, I thinned the needles and wired all the previous year's growth before the candles began to emerge. When I reached the top of the tree, I wired a small branch upward to increase the height. By doing so, it seemed to make a gap near the top more obvious. This short area of trunk had no branches and now that the foliage had been thinned out was an obvious problem. I decided that it could be improved by carefully "ripping" a back branch near the top so that it could fill this space. In late summer the trunk was split next to the branch, using some large root pruners. After being tightly bound with wet raffia to prevent it from snapping, the branch was pulled down and held in position with thick wire. The branch continued growing happily and the apex remained healthy — problem solved!

Early Summer Year 1: **With some candle pinching, the pine foliage became denser. The tree needed to be structured.**

Summer Year 1: **Many branches were removed to further expose the trunk. I used heavy wire and a clamp to angle them horizontally.**

training tip
Quick results can be achieved by selecting heavily trunked trees with compact growth.

Late Spring Year 3: **After much thinning and more wiring, the tree's candles were pinched to encourage compact growth. The trunk top now showed a gap, which was no longer hidden by foliage.**

Over the years the bark has developed well, helping the tree achieve a look of maturity. By finding such excellent material, with many useful low branches on a powerful trunk, an impressive bonsai has been created in a relatively short space of time. As the years progress and the pads develop further, the pine will become a large, imposing bonsai.

Spring Year 8: **This close-up shows how the pine's trunk top was split and a branch torn downward, enabling the branch position to be considerably lowered, thus filling an unsightly gap.**

Spring Year 8: **Each autumn I thin the needles so maximum light reaches the buds as they form for the spring. I remove all downward-growing needles to define the foliage areas and improve the general appearance. The candles are allowed to extend and just as they begin to open, I pinch them back hard.**

Style: Formal upright
Height: 43¼ in (110cm)

literati-style scotch pine

Pinus sylvestris

Asked by a local bonsai society to carry out a styling demonstration for a forthcoming meeting, I decided to select some material that would be readily available to most members and set off for my local garden center. With no fixed ideas for raw material, I was determined to purchase a tree of some kind that day. The conifer section was stocked with a good choice of Scotch pines. They were all quite large and bushy, but one in particular caught my eye. It was growing in a large plastic bag and had more branches than the others. This was to be my demonstration tree.

Several months later the meeting arrived and I had already spent time studying the tree, planning the style and shape that I wanted to create. I chose to emulate a natural pine tree in the literati style, with a long trunk and foliage near the top. At that time I had no literati-style trees in my collection and thought that this tree could be my first. Prior to the meeting, I had looked at many pictures of such trees in bonsai books and also gazed up at several large specimens growing in the wild nearby.

As my demonstration began, I explained my thought process and started by removing all branches that were definitely not required, so that I could see more clearly what remained. Having a good mental picture of the end result, I enjoyed the gasps in the audience as the large branches were pruned off. I left potential jins in many places, since I thought they could always be trimmed off afterward.

With much unnecessary clutter removed, I thinned out the end growth on the branches, cutting out every strong central shoot on each group of three to balance the growth and promote budding. The top of the tree was rather leggy and needed shortening.

With so many suitable branches available, a new leader was easily selected and the overall height was reduced considerably. Every branch was then wired and I avoided trapping needles where possible. At this stage I had not shaped anything and the tree was now ready for branch placement, which for me is the most enjoyable part of styling. I began moving the main branches upward, treating them as separate trunks high up in the tree, the way Scotch pine trees so often grow in nature. After arranging the secondary branches, the initial styling was complete. Although the pine was a long way from being a bonsai tree, the future shape had been outlined and the demonstration was well received and appreciated.

In the spring I removed the tree from the bag and carefully teased out the thick roots, making the root system more shallow. After some minor root pruning, the tree was planted in a wooden training box that I had constructed. To help the pine recover and gain strength, I allowed the new candles to grow and extend into shoots, lightly trimming them in midsummer. After staying in the box a further year, the tree was then planted in my favorite type of bonsai container — a round drum pot. This shape of pot is ideal for a tall, thin, literati-style tree, helping the bonsai image unfold and greatly enhancing the pine's appearance.

By minimal feeding and careful watering during Years 7–9, the needle size has become smaller and more in scale with the rest of the tree. I am careful not to starve this tree though, since there is a fine line between tiny unhealthy needles and those of a perfect medium size. Being such a natural shape, this tall literati bonsai has become a miniature replica of the wild trees from which I originally drew inspiration.

Summer Year 1: **I placed the pine, bag and all, in a deep box to make it stable and easier to move.**

Winter Year 1: **The upper trunks started reverting to their previous position, so I tied them more closely to the main trunk.**

training tip

When selecting garden center stock, look for good surface roots, a well-shaped, tapering trunk and evenly distributed, compact branches.

Summer Year 2: **I trimmed new shoots and pulled out many downward needles to clearly define the branches.**

Spring Year 4: **By planting in a shallow, round pot, the tree now appeared somewhat taller and therefore more elegant.**

Late Summer Year 9: **By Year 8 the tree was in need of major refinement. I took the opportunity to remove many branches that were now unnecessary. After some needle pulling, wiring and positioning, the image has improved immensely.**

Style: Literati
Height: 35in (89cm)

informal upright scotch pine

Pinus sylvestris

Over the years I have been lucky enough to become good friends with the staff at my local wholesale nursery. With more than 20 acres of plants, either in pots or growing in the open ground, I am often allowed to wander the whole site when looking for potential bonsai material. On this particular occasion, one summer's morning, I was walking around the nursery hoping to find a large pine tree. At this time I had few pines in my collection and wanted the opportunity to further my knowledge of this species. Noticing a row of very large pines lined up alongside a truck, I went to investigate. They were all Scotch pines, apparently destined for a nearby golf course. Most were clearly not suitable for bonsai training, being too tall and lacking lower branches. I spotted one, however, which looked very appealing. Despite being over 6½ft (2m) tall, its thick trunk contained many small branches lower down. The bark had an aged appearance and I persuaded the manager that this tree should come home with me. With a little friendly negotiation, we agreed on a very favorable price (for me), and I loaded the pine into my trailer, which I had brought in case.

One Sunday morning during the winter, I was invited to a fellow enthusiast's house for a "bonsai day" with several other keen bonsai growers. I decided to style this pine, which I thought would keep me busy, and indeed spent the whole day working my way up the tree, wiring and shaping each branch as I went. Pines have the great advantage of being very flexible and I was able to successfully reposition some fairly thick branches.

In the spring the pine was planted in a training box and positioned in full sunlight. After some candle pinching, small buds started to form on the branches much closer to the trunk. I could not prune these branches back to the more suitable buds yet, since the end shoots of the branch were required to keep the sap flowing. Pruning at this stage would have killed the new buds, so I waited patiently for one year, then reduced the length of many of these long branches. The pine was completely structured and all the branches were rewired. Unfortunately, the main and most important branch on the tree had not budded back and was spoiling the overall appearance. Because the tree was an evergreen and the branches would never be seen without foliage, I was able to employ an interesting technique to improve this branch. The shoots were twisted, coiled and "snaked" to shorten them and bring the foliage closer together. Some growth was bent back toward the trunk, filling in the bare areas of the branch. Although at this stage it was obvious what I had done, I was confident that in several years the branch would be dense and this twisted structure completely hidden from view by lush foliage. The tree remained in the box for a further two years.

After over four years of training, the branches of the pine were still not as dense as I had hoped and so I planted the tree in the garden to

Autumn Year 1: **The lower branches needed more energy and light, as they were beginning to die back, so I sawed off the top two-thirds of the tree, which was also making the tall pine top-heavy.**

Autumn Year 1: **With top removed, the tree was more stable. I picked a small side branch to become the new leader. I was confident that, with time, a good crown could be shaped.**

Early Spring Year 2: **I made a large box in which I planted the tree for training, and I fed it heavily. As candles grew, I pinched them back to encourage budding.**

Summer Year 7: **To encourage stronger, denser growth, I planted the pine in the garden. The only training was candle pinching in spring. Where necessary, some were allowed to extend more than others.**

grow further. I fed it regularly to promote vigorous growth and it responded well. After the pine had been growing in the ground for three years, I planted it in a bonsai pot. The roots were very healthy, being covered in beneficial white mycorrhizal fungus, which helps them absorb nutrients. Further wiring was carried out, partly flattening out the foliage so that the spring candles could begin to create well-shaped pads. Downward-growing needles were pulled out to give the branches clean lines and the apex was thinned extensively in order to reduce its vigor.

Looking back, I consider myself most fortunate that I visited the nursery on that particular day. Had it been just one day later, this impressive and individual bonsai would have been just another pine tree growing on a golf course.

Early Spring Year 9: **When I planted this tree in a bonsai pot, I was surprised at how large it had become. The pine needed a good deal of work to redefine the foliage masses, which were rather overgrown.**

Summer Year 9: **Foliage has been strategically placed to camouflage the top where the trunk diameter changes. The new leader has thickened considerably and the original pruning is becoming less obvious. I pinch the outer candles hardest, leaving them longer toward the center of each branch so that the foliage pads are not flat but raised and domed.**

Style: Informal upright
Height: 37in (94cm)

rescued blackthorn

Prunus spinosa

One winter morning I had the good fortune to notice a local farmer removing a small section of his hedge and replacing it with a gate. I spotted a blackthorn with an interesting trunk lying among the pile of trees that he intended to burn. The farmer seemed quite surprised when I asked if I could have it and said that I was welcome to take whatever I wanted. I happily returned home with my tree.

The roots were badly damaged by the tree having been ripped from the ground. I pruned them back neatly and painted the cuts with wound sealant to prevent disease. At this stage the trunk was also heavily pruned to 10 in (25cm), since the growth above this point was uninteresting and lacked appeal. A small side branch became the new leader and the tree was planted in the front garden to recover. That year it grew strongly, and by lightly pruning all side growth, I forced the blackthorn to direct all its energy into the new leader so that it would thicken and the cut would become less obvious. It soon reached almost 6½ft (2m) in height and the tree seemed to be growing well.

The next year, to create good taper, I pruned the new growth down to 6in (15cm) and trained another side branch up as the leader, which was allowed to grow unchecked for the rest of the season.

After the blackthorn had been in the garden for two years, I reduced the height once more by about four-fifths and pruned the branches back to begin its training in a box. Normally when trees grow, every shoot that extends corresponds to a root growing. I was completely amazed when I discovered that the tree's roots were virtually unchanged from when it had been planted in the garden so long ago. How had it been possible for this tree to make so much growth with such poor roots? I immediately potted it into a square box, using a very free-draining mix of mainly grit and akadama, hoping that this soil would promote fibrous roots.

The tree budded well and I let the shoots develop, wiring several in place to establish a definite branch structure. I fed it heavily, but did not prune the growth since I was conscious that the roots were poor and needed to recover. The next spring, to my relief and joy, the tree had become so potbound with fibrous roots that it was difficult to remove from the box. A large bonsai pot was selected, the blackthorn was root pruned and wired, and the trunk angle was slightly changed. I wondered whether it would flower that spring, but was not surprised when none appeared. Now that the tree was strong, with a healthy root system, I pruned off many unnecessary branches and wired the remaining shoots into a tree-like structure. In the autumn I fed it with bonemeal in an attempt to promote flowers. The following spring my patience was rewarded with an excellent display of small white flowers, evenly distributed among the branches. It looked an absolute picture and also flowered the following year, although not so heavily.

Two years later the tree was rather overgrown and needed some serious styling. I prefer to work on deciduous trees when they don't have leaves, because they are much easier to wire without leaves and the structure can be fully appreciated. Many branches were pruned off, since I was confident that the remaining ones I intended to use were alive. Every branch and twig was wired into shape and the blackthorn was given extra winter protection because of the pruning. I was aware that I had removed many of that year's flowers, but the shape was more important to me — there will be many more spectacular springs to look forward to.

Autumn Year 1: **By the end of the first summer in the garden, the new leader had grown astonishingly. It was thickening quite considerably.**

Spring Year 3: **The blackthorn was potted in a box and pruned hard to promote budding. The open soil mix was much better than the clay garden soil.**

Summer Year 6: **I often let a tree's shoots extend, to ensure the branches thicken. I trained a new side branch as the leader. The blackthorn began to resemble a tree.**

training tip

Allow flowering trees to become potbound in order to promote the formation of flower buds.

opposite, Summer Year 9: **A smaller, round, green-glazed pot has now been selected — a perfect match for this flowering tree. The surface roots are impressive, making the base seem solid, and balancing the curve of the trunk line.**

Style: Informal upright
Height: 19¾in (50cm)

restored
weeping willow

Salix babylonica

I had known this tree for many years before it actually came into my possession. It used to be the star tree in a friend's large collection and I often admired it when visiting. Grown for over 20 years from a very small cutting, it was displayed separately on a pedestal to allow its graceful branches plenty of room to weep and show itself to its best advantage. While on holiday for two weeks, my friend entrusted the care of his trees to his son. The weather was hot and frequent watering ensured that the trees remained healthy. During the second week, however, my friend's son realized that he had not even noticed the willow at the other end of the garden. The pot had been placed in a dish of water, which was now completely dry. All the tree's leaves were dried up and brown — it was a total disaster. The willow was immediately watered but did not appear to revive and looked very sorry for itself indeed.

Upon my friend's return his son explained what had happened. On close inspection the majority of the branches were dying back, but being a vigorous species, there was certainly hope. The tree was moved to a shady area of the garden, where it continued to die back. One branch remained alive and new shoots soon appeared at the end of it and at the base of the dead branches. All was not lost, but it would be several years before this tree was returned to its former glory.

Summer Year 1: **Despite its overgrown appearance, the tree had a substantial, well-shaped trunk and a good flare at the base.**

I acquired the willow six months later, after its health had been restored through tender care and regular feeding. My friend had lost enthusiasm for this tree and was therefore quite happy to sell it to me. I could not believe my good fortune, given that I had always coveted it. Having two other large willows in my bonsai collection, I was confident that it would not be long before this tree was looking as good as those, particularly since the excess growth had resulted in a thickening of the trunk.

Autumn Year 1: **To establish a structure, I pruned most new branches hard. I left a smaller one untouched to help it strengthen and thicken.**

Late Spring Year 2: **I changed the angle slightly, potting it more upright. After cutting back all the branches and wiring some, buds appeared all over.**

Summer Year 2: **In summer, I fed the tree well and stood it in a dish of water. New shoots were wired down to encourage weeping in an arching manner.**

Early Spring Year 3: **Planted in a new pot, the tree was pruned hard and an arching structure started to form. I allowed a new leader to develop, to increase the height.**

I repotted the tree the following spring. It was completely potbound, so much so that the pot had begun to crack in several places, and I strengthened it by applying epoxy to the inside. The roots were pruned heavily and all the branches cut back. I removed the final remaining original branch, replacing it with a new, more suitable, smaller shoot, and the tree grew strongly. In the following spring, the willow was planted in a new, slightly larger, more elegant pot and pruned hard.

After just two years the willow looked glorious. I keep this tree in light shade, which certainly helps it stay healthy and very green. This weeping willow managed to survive its ordeal, and as the gradual arching of the branches develops, it will without doubt get better and better every year.

training tip
Willows should always be pruned hard each spring and the branches wired and trained to keep downward once they are long enough. This is an annual exercise.

Summer Year 3: **The structure had developed well and the overall appearance was balanced. Each shoot was wired vertically to ensure a uniform weeping habit. On a small scale, weeping willows need great encouragement to weep.**

Style: Weeping
Height: 34in (86cm)

weeping willow cutting

Salix babylonica

This was one of the very first trees I trained as a bonsai. I was aware that willow branches were easy to root and pruned a small branch from a friend's weeping willow one spring, as the buds were beginning to open. It quickly rooted in a bucket of water and was then potted into a flower pot where it grew well in its first year.

The next spring I planted the willow in a shallow, round bonsai pot. I had no experience or knowledge of how to treat this variety and for the next two years I thoughtlessly pinched the growing tips to stop them from becoming long.

After this time I decided that the tree would benefit from being planted in a large flower pot and it responded well to this extra space for root growth. A new leader was wired upward to increase the height and in the summer I sat the pot in a saucer of water.

Although the willow had grown well, the trunk was still fairly thin, and I now decided that I wanted a larger tree than I had previously envisioned. In the spring it was planted in a garden border and staked with a cane. It was watered well during dry periods and produced an explosion of growth. I was conscious that the trunk was lacking taper and utilized a small shoot near the base to grow as a "sacrifice" branch. The top of the tree was then pruned heavily to direct energy toward this small shoot, which quickly began to grow. I also trimmed all the side branches before they became too thick, to avoid large pruning scars.

After spending less than four years in the ground, the willow had reached a height of over 6ft (1.8m) and was beginning to take over the garden. The trunk had thickened considerably and the bark was starting to look older and less smooth at the base. It was time to lift it from the ground and continue its training in a bonsai pot.

In the spring the soil was washed away from the roots, uncovering a tangled mass that I pruned heavily. All branches were removed, including the

Late Spring Year 2: **After a year in a flower pot, I potted the willow in a small dish.**

thick sacrifice branch at the back of the tree which had served its purpose, revealing a well-shaped, tapering trunk line. I planted the tree in a large, round bonsai pot and buds quickly emerged all up the trunk. Many were rubbed off and I selected those best positioned to become large branches, allowing them to grow. I fed it heavily and stood the pot in a dish of water. By early summer the growth was long enough to shape and I wired each branch, arching them downward so that they were completely vertical. The shoot tips were pruned to prevent them continuing to grow and spoiling the shape. A solid yet very appealing weeping willow bonsai had emerged.

Summer Year 4: **I allowed the willow, now in a large pot, to grow long shoots. The trunk was reluctant to thicken.**

Late Summer Year 8: **After growing in the ground for 3½ years, the willow was overgrown, despite being pruned back repeatedly.**

Early Spring Year 9: **After lifting, I cut the height down to about one-third and removed all branches, including the sacrifice branch.**

Late Spring Year 9: **Now branchless, the trunk quickly produced a mass of buds, providing many branch positions to choose from.**

Summer Year 9: **All branches and shoots are wired vertically to create a weeping image. Each spring they will be pruned back to just a few buds and regrown to slowly develop the arching branch structure.**

Style: Weeping
Height: 31½ in (80cm)

stately styrax

Styrax japonica

One late spring at a bonsai society meeting I noticed a very eye-catching tree in full flower. On inquiring as to the species I was informed that this bonsai was a styrax. The flowers resembled snowdrops, which the owner told me turn into grayish, round berries in the autumn as an added attraction, but, on the downside, the styrax has a tendency for branches to die back in the winter. Although very attractive in flower, the bonsai was nevertheless poorly designed with a heavily curved S-shaped trunk. I decided that my collection was definitely lacking a styrax and that I would begin a search for a suitable specimen.

I was always on the lookout for such a tree when visiting bonsai nurseries, but the only styrax I ever saw also had ugly, unnatural 'S'-shaped trunks. Later that year, a friend told me about a bonsai nursery that was importing two very large potential specimen styrax in the spring. One had a hollow trunk, which he had selected for himself. The other tree of equal quality could be saved for me on a first-refusal basis. I jumped at this opportunity and eagerly awaited their arrival during the winter.

Soon the phone call came to say that our trees were waiting at the nursery for our inspection. We drove up together the next day and made sure that there was plenty of room in the back of the car for our trees, should we decide to buy them. When I first saw these styrax bonsai, I was amazed at the size of the trunks. I had never seen styrax that were so big and was told by the nursery owner that, being this large, they were two very unusual trees. My friend's tree was the smaller of the two and its main attraction was a beautifully carved trunk and well-developed branches. My tree was completely different, much larger and with a poorer branch structure. This did not deter me since I wanted to

design my own tree around its powerful trunk. That afternoon we set off for home, heavily loaded with bags of akadama, our styrax trees and also several other bonsai — we had struck a very good deal. I anticipated late spring with great excitement, when I hoped the tree would be covered with flowers.

On the weekend I decided to repot the tree since it was clearly potbound, and also to change the front to a more pleasing angle. The soil still contained clay from the field where it had spent its early years and this was removed. The pot was very "incurved" and I was dismayed to see that the inside was flaking badly, making the sides of the pot very thin in places. Epoxy was applied to strengthen the pot and when this had dried, I completed the repotting process, returning the styrax to my cold greenhouse to give it good winter protection, since styrax are slightly tender trees. When placing it on the bench, one of the feet fell off the bottom of the pot. Worse still, when the tree began to grow, it became clear that over half the branches were completely dead. I was not too concerned about the pot and glued the foot back on — another pot could always be found. I was, however, worried about this unique tree and anxiously waited to see how or if it would recover.

In a matter of weeks new shoots had appeared at the bases of the dead branches and, as the temperature was now warmer, the bonsai with its fresh new leaves was moved to a sheltered site outside. I was horrified the next day when I noticed that it had dropped a large number of leaves and thought that it must have been the shock of moving it, even though it was very mild by now. More leaves continued to fall for the next few weeks before the tree started to recover. When I was happy that the tree was growing strongly and that no flowers were going to appear, I pruned, wired and set in place a basic branch structure. The tree grew well that summer.

After good winter protection, the next year I decided to leave the tree in the greenhouse for longer in spring (Year 2), so that it would be stronger before moving it outside.

Early Spring Year 1: **The tree's main feature was the large trunk, which was full of character. I decided to change the front, selecting a view with a more pleasing buttress and a trunk line with better taper.**

Summer Year 1: **I let the styrax grow unchecked, to gain strength. It grew well, but there were no flowers.**

When it was in full leaf and growing well, the styrax was moved to the most sheltered area in the garden, but, as before, it proceeded to drop many leaves. A couple of small branches had also died and were beginning to resprout at the base. This was obviously a fussy tree, but I was in no doubt that it would be worth all the trouble, anticipating flowers that year. Unfortunately, no flowers came, although the tree continued to grow well. My friend's styrax also had yet to flower, so that was reassuring.

The next year I thought it prudent to let the styrax leaf out on the bonsai bench outside, moving it into the shed any night that frost was forecast. The tree seemed much stronger when the leaves arrived, and not one fell off. I think that I had been cosseting this tree too much. A major branch had died during the winter, but again there was a young shoot nearby to replace it. The bonsai was looking healthier than it ever had and then, to my delight, it flowered for the first time. What a joy! I was confident that the tree would flower well from now on, but that was not the case. One year later, although still in good health, only three flowers appeared. Maybe the tree was growing too well at the expense of flowers.

On a regular visit to a local bonsai nursery to stock up on spring supplies, I noticed a wonderful, large, oval pot at the top of a bonsai pot display. I commented to my wife that it would suit the styrax, and since that morning another foot had fallen off the existing pot, I decided that the bonsai had reached a stage where it really deserved a better, larger pot. With this new pot giving greater room for root development, the frustrating problem of shedding branches during the winter might be resolved. I am convinced that the small pot was the cause of the trouble and that the tree will now be much happier with the additional room for root growth. On arrival home, the styrax was root pruned hard and planted in the new pot. The transformation was simply tremendous.

Summer Year 2: **To encourage flowering, I fed it heavily with high potash fertilizer throughout the year. The top became vigorous and was pruned hard, directing energy to the lower branches, but, still no flowers.**

Early Summer Year 3: **With many white bell-shaped flowers, the styrax was a sight to behold. Berries soon followed. I looked forward to even more flowers over the years to follow.**

opposite, Summer Year 6: **Despite flowering well the year before, only three flowers appeared this summer. The branches were developing well, however, and, even without flowers, this tree was becoming quite impressive.**

right, Early Spring Year 7: **The new pot was an excellent match. The bonsai appears much larger and more imposing, enhancing the tree's strong winter image. Equally important, the pot has four solid feet, showing no signs of falling off, and so stability was also improved. Hopefully, the pot will have a positive effect on the tree by making it flower well again.**

Style: Informal upright
Height: 30in (76cm)

driftwood wisteria

Wisteria sinensis

This was my first attempt at creating the illusion of an ancient bonsai tree from a piece of driftwood and a whippy young plant. Considering all the suitable species, I decided on wisteria because they are easy to obtain, reasonably priced and, with time, produce a profusion of colorful flowers. I envisioned a breathtaking image of a heavily trunked tree, covered in beautiful racemes of long, flowing, purple flowers.

While visiting a garden center on holiday in the summer, I noticed an exquisite piece of driftwood that was being sold for decoration in aquariums. I instantly thought that this piece of root looked very tree-like and when I began handling it, I started thinking of how stunning it would be if it were the trunk of a wisteria bonsai. It was certainly most suitable for a "wrap-around" project, and I walked around outside, searching for a plant that could possibly be attached to the wood. Outside, there were many wisteria and I chose the one with the least ugly graft.

Early Autumn Year 1: **This young wisteria, with its thin, flexible trunk, was the ideal candidate for a "wrap-around."**

The driftwood was soaked in a bucket of clear wood preserver for three months and then left outside in the winter, allowing the rain to wash the potential "trunk." During this time, I made a double-thickness chicken-wire base for the wood. I drilled small holes near the bottom of the driftwood so that it could be fastened onto the base with wire ties, to give the wood more stability. Epoxy was then spread over the wire base to make it solid. As spring began to approach, I painted the brown driftwood with lime sulfur three times, waiting for sunny days so that it would dry well and to give it a bleached effect. I carved a small channel around the back of the trunk, where the wisteria would be attached.

The roots were in good condition when I removed the wisteria from its flower pot. Using a sharp knife, I cut a strip of bark from the plant, so that when growing up the driftwood, the resulting callus would help it form a strong attachment. This is where things began to go wrong! As I started to bend and manipulate the wisteria to follow the contours of the prepared channel around the wood, the bark showed signs of coming away from the center wood. Before I knew it, the bark actually bowed and separated completely from the trunk. I was rather alarmed at this and quickly put them back together. I then secured the wisteria to the

Summer Year 2: **Just three months after its creation, the wisteria looked like an old tree. I let it grow for the rest of the year so it could gain much-needed strength.**

Spring Year 4: **Now heavily wired, the tree began to acquire a definite structure. The new pot was more suitable, blending well with the color of the driftwood.**

Autumn Year 6: **Although flowers are undoubtedly the main feature of wisteria, the tree's strong, yellow autumn colors are also quite dramatic and provide added interest.**

Late Spring Year 8: **Now that the wisteria is flowering, it should do so each spring, with (I hope) more flowers every year. It is vital to protect from late frosts, which can cause considerable damage to flower buds.**

Style: Driftwood
Height: 26in (66cm)

wood by carefully hammering in several staples over the trunk, tied it to the wood with string and planted it in a training pot. Holding out little hope of survival, I nevertheless placed the potential bonsai in a large plastic bag in order to provide humidity, where I hoped it might recover in its own micro-environment. Thankfully, it did survive, and within six weeks the buds began to swell and new shoots emerged.

The next year the tree was lightly pruned, and wiring allowed basic branch placement. Although the branches were very young, the overall image was beginning to look quite natural and promising. I screwed the wisteria to the driftwood to create a tighter bond,

since it was starting to come away in several places. That year I purchased a rectangular, silvery gray bonsai pot, which I thought would complement the driftwood well, and I planted the tree in its new pot the following spring. I was pleased to see that the roots had grown well, but did not root-prune because I wanted the wisteria to remain fairly pot-bound in the hope of encouraging flowers, although none came. I was not disheartened since the wisteria was very young — even when grafted, they can often take many years to flower.

Three years later, and after much wiring and pruning in late summer, I was rewarded that spring with a display of just three purple

flowers. I was so excited by their arrival that I exhibited the tree at a large bonsai show the following week, where I enjoyed overhearing comments about the bonsai. Most people believed it was actually a real tree and it was very satisfying to have created this convincing, ancient-looking wisteria bonsai in such a short space of time.

training tip
When attaching saplings to driftwood, use screws that will eventually rust away. Do not use any screw that contains copper, since this is toxic.

display

A good, healthy bonsai is always a pleasure to behold, but when it is prepared properly for exhibition, it truly becomes a thing of beauty. The hobby takes on another dimension when showing bonsai in public, and it is worth striving to present the tree with a perfectly refined image. A display of bonsai in the garden is highly satisfying for the owner, who can enjoy them without the need for the trees to be kept immaculately groomed.

displaying bonsai in your home

Throughout the year there will be times when your bonsai trees look at their absolute best — they may have fresh new leaves, flowers, a good crop of fruit, fantastic autumn colors, striking winter structure or have recently been trimmed. These are ideal times to enjoy one tree away from the rest of the collection. Display it in a cool, uncluttered part of the house for no more than one or two days, to avoid stressing the bonsai. Select an area against a plain background where the structure of the tree can be fully appreciated. The site should also be away from heat sources, such as radiators.

In Japan, bonsai has become an important part of life and an area of the house is frequently set aside for viewing the bonsai in isolation, often an alcove. This display consists of three elements: the bonsai tree (man), a scroll (heaven) and an accessory (earth), and this symbolic triangle is known as a *tokonoma*. The scroll is positioned centrally and should be subtle and understated, complementing the tree. Most often, the ornament accessory is an accent planting (*see* pages 134–35) or viewing stone (*suiseki*). When viewed as a whole, the arrangement should portray a feeling of complete unity, rather than three separate items grouped together. Although it is difficult to create an authentic *tokonoma* area, by understanding and employing the main principles of harmony, balance and simplicity, a bonsai display can be greatly enhanced.

right: **This Chinese elm is pictured here in a typical *tokonoma* setting.**

displaying bonsai at exhibitions

Exhibiting bonsai trees in public is often the culmination of many years of training and can be a very proud and satisfying moment for experienced exhibitors and novice enthusiasts alike, who are usually encouraged to share their trees with others. The venue may be in a flower tent at a local horticultural show, a society display staged in a school hall or at a national exhibition in a large venue. Whatever the case, it provides the chance to encourage and educate other bonsai enthusiasts, while also promoting the hobby. Take the time to study other trees at eye level. What makes them a successful or poor bonsai? What techniques have been used in their training? How long have they been in training? Where possible, bonsai should be displayed against a plain background, untextured and neutral in color. To display bonsai at their absolute best and to ensure the most effective presentation requires meticulous preparation prior to the exhibition.

above: **A bonsai in full flower can be spectacular and provides tremendous interest and appeal when exhibited, as in the case of this** *Gaultheria mucronata.* **Grown from nursery stock eight years ago, it flowers for several weeks each summer, when it has been shown on several occasions.**

exhibiting guidelines

• Ensure that the soil surface is free from weeds, dead leaves and other debris. Remove the top ⅜ in (1cm) of soil and replace with finely sieved Japanese akadama clay. The soil should be level with the sides of the pot, mounding up slightly to the buttress.

• Underplant with a selection of moss, forming a green "island" around the base of the tree but not completely covering the soil, to create a natural landscaped look. Use a variety of different-sized mosses to emulate the many colors and contours of plants that grow underneath trees in the wild, trimming off moss seeds with scissors. Accentuate the surface roots by carefully positioning moss on either side of some roots, and if possible, cover any ugly roots that spoil the overall appearance.

• Use a toothbrush to clean off unsightly algae and surface lichens from trunks and branches. Show the buttress to its best advantage by ensuring that it is fully exposed, together with all surface roots. Trim any visible root hairs that may be sticking up out of the soil.

• Remove any unnecessary wires, ties and clamps. Remaining wire should be very neat and discreet. Avoid silver wire unless the tree is to be exhibited in an educational "trees in training" display. Make sure that the tree is completely stable in its pot and that any tying wires are not visible.

• The bonsai must always be in excellent health and free from pests and diseases. Feed several weeks in advance so that the foliage is a healthy green color and showing no signs of nutrient deficiency.

• At least two days before exhibiting, clean the pot with water, and when dry, carefully wipe unglazed or dull pots with a small amount of oil to improve the color. A very fine oil such as wood-scratch remover is ideal, since this is unlikely to attract dust. Do allow time for the oil to soak in.

• Define foliage masses by trimming downward growth. For pines, cedars and larches, remove any downward-pointing needles by carefully pulling them out. Groom branches by pruning overgrown shoots to shape and thin growth — ideally, most foliage pads should be made up from smaller masses. Carry out any leaf pruning at least six weeks before the exhibition, so that the tree has fully leafed out, but no later than early summer. Remove any damaged, oversized or dead leaves and protect delicate trees from strong winds and scorching sunshine, so that leaves remain in good condition.

• Where possible, display the tree on a suitable wooden bonsai stand. Powerful trees are well suited to strong, solid tables and more informal trees favor slightly delicate stands. Conifers are best complemented by dark wood stands and deciduous trees look better when a lighter shade of wood is used. A "slice" of polished tree trunk, a piece of stained wood, natural slate, woven bamboo or raffia matting or even painted styrofoam blocks can all be effective. Well matched with the bonsai, a stand helps complete the picture.

• Do not use ornaments, such as figures or animals. A good bonsai should not need these to provide the illusion of scale, and they take focus away from the actual tree.

• If possible, select an appropriate accent planting or rock that reflects the character and mood of the tree without overpowering it — *see* pages 134–35.

• Over-exhibiting can be very damaging, since the environment, changing temperatures and the build-up of dust may prove stressful for the bonsai. After the exhibition, water it well from above to thoroughly wash the leaves.

accent plantings

Accent or "companion" plantings, as they are sometimes known, are grown to complement bonsai trees when being exhibited. They are placed near the bonsai and often reflect the tree's character, adding a natural element to the display. For example, a plant slightly pendulous in growth habit may be suitable when displayed next to a weeping willow. Tall, narrow literati trees are enhanced with slender grasses, which mirror the mood of the tree and suggest scale, while a much thicker-trunked, heavily barked pine would look effective next to a rough piece of stone displayed in a shallow *suiban* filled with fine sand or water. A strong feeling of season can also be represented by using small spring bulbs, summer-flowering herbs, plants with autumn colors or, in winter, grasses that are beginning to die back.

A good accent plant can be charming in its own right and may be displayed individually or as part of a group. However, when next to a bonsai tree it must not be overpowering or become the dominant feature. Good health is also essential. A yellow, deficient grass will draw attention to itself, but so will a very lush specimen grass that is unusually large and robust. Mixed accent plantings using different species in the same pot can be effective, but also difficult to create — it is often not practical to combine plants that require different growing conditions. More frequently just one plant is used, possibly underplanted with moss or similar ground cover. Growing an accent plant directly on a rock can also be pleasing, appearing natural and realistic.

Accent plants are very quick to mature and easy to create, adding another aspect to the hobby. Both plant and pot being relatively small, they also have the added advantage of being fairly inexpensive. A good way to achieve quick results is to purchase three small plants at minimal cost and plant them all closely together in one pot. This ensures the appearance of an established plant in no time at all.

So many different species and varieties of plants are suitable for accent plantings that the possibilities are almost endless and it becomes a matter of individual choice. Even plants normally considered to be weeds can be utilized to good effect. There is only one drawback to having a collection of accent plants — in your enthusiasm, you can end up with more accents than actual bonsai trees!

above right: **Blood grass — *Imperata cylindrica* — is a popular subject for cultivation by bonsai enthusiasts.**

right: **The flowers on this *Parahebe lyallii* are subtle and the dark burgundy shoot tips are reflected in the color of the pot.**

maintenance

Growing in such small containers, it is vital that accent plants are repotted each year, and the ideal time for this is early spring. Root pruning is beneficial, providing valuable space for the roots to grow and develop. Many grasses and similar plants respond well to being cut back when repotted, which activates dormant buds. Also, by removing all old and damaged foliage at this time, more air and light is able to reach the new shoots, which encourages fresh growth. Add slow-release fertilizer to the soil mix and feed throughout the summer as required, to ensure steady growth and optimum health.

Most accents should be treated as fairly short-lived and it is a good idea to plant them in the garden after two or three years, where they can become stock plants and used to propagate further accents or, indeed, garden plants.

plants suitable for accent plantings

grasses
bamboos
sedges
reeds/rushes
herbs
herbaceous plants
small shrubs
ferns
dwarf bulbs
alpine plants
moss plantings
wildflowers
garden weeds
houseplants

top: **This grass is very overgrown and in need of repotting, which will help it remain healthy.**

above: **After removing all the old foliage and root pruning, the grass was replanted in the same pot, in which it quickly began to grow.**

left: **Five months after repotting, this grass has responded well with fresh new growth. It now looks its best, covered in dainty, arching seedheads.**

displaying bonsai in your garden

Bonsai trees, however they are displayed, add interest and appeal to any garden. Position your trees in a prominent area where they can be fully enjoyed and appreciated rather than hiding them away in a corner, where out of sight they can easily become dry. They need good light and air circulation, and should be regularly turned to ensure that each part of the tree receives its fair share of sunlight, necessary for even growth and for preventing die-back.

Some of my trees are displayed on a simple wooden bench, which is stained dark brown to help it blend into the background (*see* photograph below). A bench or staging should ideally allow the bonsai to be displayed at eye level, where the trees can be viewed to their best advantage. My bonsai trees are positioned so that I am able to sit in the house, in a strategically placed armchair, and enjoy them by looking through the patio doors.

adding japanese elements

When displayed in a Japanese-style setting, bonsai trees are greatly enhanced in appearance and the overall effect can be breathtaking. Most bonsai enthusiasts add Japanese touches to their gardens. These can be very effective and need not be expensive or difficult to achieve, as the following photographs of my garden illustrate.

Siting bonsai on separate wooden plinths is a wonderful way to display individual trees in the garden. With clean, simple lines they are an excellent alternative to benching and can be used to display either single specimens or groups of bonsai trees. Sections of telephone poles create an imaginative alternative pedestal upright (*see* page 138, bottom photograph). These are highly suitable for displaying cascade-style bonsai trees.

below: **This is a perfect area in which to grow my trees, since a variety of conditions are available. The right-hand side is shaded by a large oak tree and provides a very different micro-environment to that of the left-hand side. Along the bench, the light ranges from full sun through to medium shade.**

The addition of Japanese lanterns in the garden instantly creates an oriental atmosphere. Lanterns made of reconstituted stone are a much cheaper alternative to granite. In humid environments, moss soon sprouts on the porous surface, giving the lantern an old and weathered appearance.

My bonsai workshop, housed in a shed, was unattractive and in a dull corner of the garden, but with very little expenditure and a weekend's work, this eyesore was transformed into a real feature. A pergola was created around two sides of the shed.

left: **These stands are made from fencing posts with rectangular slatted table tops, constructed using short lengths of wood and stained dark brown. The ground has been mulched with slate chippings, underlaid with matting to deter weeds. When it rains, the slate changes from gray to an attractive deep purple color.**

below: **This willow (*Salix babylonica*) is ideal to stand on a separate pedestal, from which its branches weep gracefully downward.**

Wisteria were planted around the posts and are beginning to grow well. A decking pathway, surrounded with pebbles and edged with bamboo cane 3in (7.5cm) wide, completes the picture.

Plants are a very important element in a Japanese-style garden, and if you could grow only a few types, then maples, bamboos and pines would be an absolute must. They are all strongly architectural plants and provide year-round interest, with the maples producing fantastic autumn color. Several maples growing in my garden were originally propagated by air layering and at the beginning were destined to be trained as bonsai trees. However, I decided that they would look best in the garden and are now becoming large trees.

We all have bonsai that we do not know what to do with. Maybe they will never make good bonsai for one reason or another. I have planted several of my trees in a pebble "beach" that surrounds one side of my pond, where they are trained as "garden" bonsai, together with other plants such as hebes, which form a natural ball of foliage reminiscent of clipped azaleas often found in Japanese gardens. Many trees in my garden started life as bonsai; some are kept pruned, while others are allowed to grow much larger. This is a great way to reduce a collection, but still keep the trees.

above: **Using black and red wood stains further enhanced the Japanese flavor of my revamped garden shed.**

left: **This five-tier pagoda is the perfect backdrop and looks wonderful at night when the candles inside are lit. Its base is softened by a privet plant (*Ligustrum ovalifolium*) with the foliage clipped into round ball shapes, and a bamboo has been planted in close proximity.**

left: This pebble beach provides an ideal setting for bonsai trees that I no longer want in my collection, but for sentimental reasons wish to keep — and because they are reasonable trees. The upright rock makes an intriguing water feature.

below: The fern garden is set off to best effect with modern, green glass gravel — broken glass that has been processed to remove the sharp edges. Stone balls provide the spherical shapes often associated with Japanese gardens. A large pine tree is hung with heavy, black iron lanterns to weigh the branches downward, while solar-powered lights provide gentle light once the sun sets.

Stepping stones are both practical and ornamental. Well positioned, they can provide a natural-looking pathway around the garden. The manmade variety offers a practical alternative to real stone, and is very convincing (*see* photograph above). They are relatively inexpensive and readily available at many garden centers.

No Japanese-style garden is complete without the addition of water in some form. I acquired a rock that was highly fissured and most interesting. When I was first positioning it in the garden I washed it thoroughly and noticed that water could run through a small hole near the top. Capitalizing on this, I situated the rock above a small reservoir made with an old piece of pond liner and now trickle water through this hole and down the front of the rock with the aid of a small capacity pump (*see* photograph above). This is most effective and provides the gentle, relaxing sound of running water.

On a larger scale, I created a koi pond in my garden, measuring over 22ft (6.5m) long, 15ft (4.5m) wide by 5ft (1.5m) deep. Approximately 55 tons (56 tonnes) of soil were removed using a small mechanical digger hired for the weekend, the assistance of many friends and much hard work. The pond contains approximately 5,000 gallons (22,700 liters) of water and 20 fish. Koi carp are demanding, fussy fish that require filtration at all times to maintain high water quality. My four filter bays are neatly hidden behind the nearby shed. These delightful fish are not only colorful and fast-growing, but inquisitive and most entertaining. They can quickly be tamed and soon become accustomed to feeding directly from the hand.

left: **With vertical sides, deep water and a surrounding wall, herons will be unable to wade into the pond and therefore my precious fish will be safe.**

below: **Koi are very destructive and will not allow most underwater aquatic plants to grow. Instead of having a marginal shelf, planting baskets containing reeds and irises have been fixed to the retaining wall.**

above: **Introducing Japanese characters can add authenticity to a garden, such as this engraved stone. Stenciling garden furniture can also be effective.**

above right: **This metal lantern is highly oriental in design. As it ages, the surface will begin to rust and take on a pleasing antiqued appearance.**

Additional details can help set the tone of the whole garden. These can include underplantings of black mondo grass, dwarf bamboo or plaques, dragons, bamboo deer-scarers, Buddhas and many other decorative items. Positioned subtly in the garden, they add extra interest when happened upon.

right: **Bamboo canes can be utilized in various ways. Here they provide an effective and attractive border edging.**

addresses glossary

The American Bonsai Society, Inc.

c/o Patricia DeGroot

ABS Executive Secretary

PO Box 1136

Puyallup, WA 98371-1136

website: www.absbonsai.org

Bonsai Clubs International

BCI Business Office

Metairie, LA 70011-8445

fax: (504) 834 2298

website: www.bonsai-bci.com

Toronto Bonsai Society

PO Box 155

Don Mills, ON M3C 2R6

tel: (416) 661-0620

website: www.tbs.game2.com

Contact the Author

email: martin_treasure@hotmail.com

above: **This silver birch (*Betula pendula*) was originally collected from the wild and has a very natural appearance.**

accent plant

A separate plant or group of plants used to add a subtle element of nature when exhibiting bonsai trees, also known as **companion plant**. Small in size, suitable plants include grasses, reeds, herbs, bulbs and many others.

air layer

Method of propagation, encouraging branches to produce roots while still attached to the tree. Achieved by ring barking an individual branch that is then wrapped in sphagnum moss and sealed within a plastic bag. When sufficient roots have grown, the branch is severed to become a new plant.

akadama

A Japanese clay produced specifically for bonsai, which is both free-draining and highly absorbent. Akadama changes color depending on water content.

anneal

To heat copper wire, making it easier to bend.

apex

The top growth or highest point on a tree.

apical bud

A bud at the tip of a shoot.

back budding

Where buds are encouraged to emerge on bare areas of branches.

bleeding

The loss of sap caused by wounding or pruning.

branch pad

The foliage mass on a branch, also known as **foliage pad**.

buttress

The base of a trunk.

callus

Woody "scar" tissue that grows over a wound.

candles

The annual new shoots found on pine trees.

canopy

Upper and outermost portion of the tree's branches.

carving

Cutting into branches or trunks, using either hand or power tools, to produce aged areas of dead wood.

chichi

Nodules found on the trunks of old ginkgo specimens.

companion plant

A separate plant or group of plants used to add a subtle element of nature when exhibiting bonsai trees, also known as **accent plant**. Small in size, suitable plants include grasses, reeds, herbs, bulbs and many others.

crown

Upper part of a tree, formed by the trunk and spreading branches.

deciduous

Tree or shrub that sheds its leaves every autumn and develops new foliage in spring.

defoliation
Leaf pruning, whereby some or all of the leaves are removed to encourage new shoots and smaller leaves on deciduous trees.

die-back
The death of shoots or branch tips, caused by drought, insects, disease, lack of light or extreme weather conditions.

dormancy
Resting period for plants, during the winter months and when little or no growth is produced.

dwarf
Variety or cultivar of a larger plant, with compact, slow growth, indicated by the Latin name *nana*.

ericaceous
Describes acidic soil conditions or a plant that requires this.

evergreen
Tree or shrub that retains its leaves throughout the year.

fibrous root
Fine roots that absorb water and nutrients from the soil.

foliage pad
The foliage mass on a branch, also known as **branch pad**.

ibigawa rock
A type of rock from the Ibigawa region of Japan with a grayish hue, it is often highly fissured and sometimes carved artificially by acid. Ideal for rock plantings.

internode
The length between sets of buds on plant growth.

jin
A branch or apex of a tree that has been stripped of bark, shaped and bleached.

leader
The main shoot at the top of a tree.

lime sulfur
Used to paint jins and deadwood areas to bleach and preserve.

mame
A miniature bonsai, which can be held in the palm of a hand.

mycorrhiza
A beneficial fungus found mainly on conifer roots, most often pines, helping them absorb nutrients.

NPK
Chemical symbols for main elements found in fertilizers:
N – nitrogen (for foliage),
P – phosphorus (for roots) and
K – potassium (for flowers).

nebari
The Japanese term for exposed surface rootage.

needle
A very narrow leaf, often evergreen and usually pointed, being hard in texture, e.g., foliage on pines and spruce trees.

node
The area of a plant stem where leaves emerge.

open soil mix
A mixture of soil with a high grit content, ensuring good drainage.

petiole
The leaf stalk.

photosynthesis
The process whereby sunlight is absorbed by plant foliage and converted into sugars by combining carbon dioxide and water.

pinching
A technique used to control and shape soft new growth, by carefully pinching or pulling off small shoots by hand.

pinnate
A leaf stem that comprises several "leaflets" on separate stalks.

raceme
A long flower stem with many separate flower stalks, e.g., wisteria flowers.

ramification
Dense, compact growth as a result of pruning techniques.

ring barking
Used in air layering, a strip of bark is removed from a branch to promote root growth at that selected point.

shari
Bleached, driftwood area of trunk, where bark has been removed.

shohin
A small-sized bonsai tree.

snaking
Technique for shortening the length of a branch by introducing acute bends, also known as **zig-zagging**. The result is that the foliage is brought closer together. Particularly useful in evergreen trees.

stratify
Natural process whereby seeds are exposed to freezing and thawing during winter, encouraging germination. These conditions can also be recreated artificially using a refrigerator or freezer.

suiban
A shallow pot without drainage holes. Used to display individual viewing stones (*see* **suiseki**), often being filled with fine sand, or for rock plantings, which are usually stood in water.

suiseki
Viewing stones that suggest a mountain scene or landscape, usually displayed in shallow pots or specially carved wooden stands.

systemic
A type of insecticide or fungicide that is absorbed into the system of a plant.

tap root
The main downward-growing root of a tree, helping to anchor it firmly in the ground.

tokonoma
An area where individual specimen bonsai are displayed, consisting of three elements: the bonsai tree (man), a scroll (heaven) and an accessory (earth).

transpiration
The natural process of water loss from the surfaces of leaves and stems of plants.

tufa rock
A type of soft limestone rock, easily carved and ideal for rock plantings.

uro
A carved or natural trunk recess area, at the point where a branch has been removed.

zig-zagging
Technique for shortening the length of a branch, by introducing acute bends, also known as **snaking**. The result is that the foliage is brought closer together. Particularly useful in evergreen trees.

index